Catherine Murray

Recipes *of a* Lifetime

A Collection *from* Readers

Wisconsin

State Journal

Copyright © 1995 Catherine Murray and the Wisconsin State Journal

Graphic Design by Daniel A. Ely

Edited by Margo O'Brien Hokanson

Coordinated by Rhonda Reese

Cover Photo by Jim Wildeman, Wildeman Photographics

Cover Photo taken at Rossario's, Monona, WI

Published by Madison Newspapers, Inc.

Printed by Straus Printing Company, Madison, Wisconsin

ISBN 1-878569-33-3

CONTENTS

INTRODUCTION

When I was a child, my imagination carried me to far away places. It also allowed me to explore with a fancy of innocence and youth the confines of Talmadge Street where I grew up. Like a child from the pages of Robert Louis Stevenson's book, "A Child's Garden of Verses," my senses were tuned to capture each moment. I sat high in the branches of our snow apple tree to gaze over adjoining backyards like a pirate in search of land. On rainy days the basement of our two-story house became Broadway where I danced in costume to 78 rpm records of Frankie Carle and other musical virtuosos on the wind-up Victrola. As a budding biologist, I searched the broken stillness of August for the cicada that hummed while perched in places I could never find. During the late evening hours, I watched shadows from the street lights dance along my bedroom wall. And I remember trying to fool the shadow that followed me wherever I went.

Life was never boring. If my imagination wasn't pumping out possibilities, I was experiencing the real thing. And while each second was savored, there was no way to predict that I would remember the ingredients that made growing up as special as it was. Children take everything for granted. Their world is made up of playtime, imagination, discoveries and learning. The mystery lies in casually remembering for a lifetime.

The field of weeds that grew along St. Paul Avenue was nothing less than magnificent. It was a hill of Let's Pretend. No colored flowers sprouted there as they do today. It was just. . . plain old weeds. . . with great hiding placed for childhood games. I ran through the field without a care in the world on paths warn thin by neighborhood playmates. When snow blanketed the weeds and the short, but steeper hill on the other side of the tracks where tiny strawberries grew wild behind Loftgordon Lumber Company, flattened cardboard boxes skimmed the surface piercing the seasonal chill with shouts of laughter until the church bells rang, reminding me and others that it was time to go home for supper.

Waiting in the background of Talmadge Street was the rest of Madison. The city was a virtual treasure chest filled with jewels for the taking. As a family, we gathered what gems we could. Pictures glued in family albums fed my memory through the years of fun that began for my sister and I in the 1930s, the decade of our births. We went everywhere with Mother and Daddy. We cooled off together in Lake Mendota at Tenney Park and ice skated its lagoons in the chill of winter. On Sundays we strolled the Vilas Park Zoo. Picnics were spread on blankets at Governor's Island and Hoyt Park. Cubes of ice kept us on track at Olbrich and Hoyt park's toboggan slides and we sledded with metal runners the vastness of the hill at Blackhawk. Indian trails led us along the edge of Lakeland Avenue and the shores of Lake Monona. Everything we did became an indelible chapter in my life.

When looking back on those wonderful days of childhood, I become aware that food played an important role in each outing. The picnic basket held Oscar Mayer wieners, Gardner's Bakery buns, Roundy's dill pickles, grocery store plums and homemade lemonade and chocolate cake, all the necessary ingredients for memorable meals in the woods. Angled wooden structures at the Vilas Park Zoo held an endless supply of Cracker Jacks and ice cream bars. After sledding, skating or tobogganing, we warmed ourselves by sipping cocoa with melting marshmallows from coffee cups with saucers. Freshly squeezed lemonade quenched our thirst after daring explorations of winding paths and rocky crevices. When the church bells rang, it was time to eat. Fifty-some years after my childhood recollections began, the Wisconsin State Journal asked if I would be interested in writing a weekly food column. The first column, scheduled for April 21, 1993, was to be an introduction for readers and what they could look forward to in Wednesday's Look section. Having to search for recipes lost or misplaced, or recipes readers wished for immediately set my mind in motion and returned me to Talmadge Street and the route from home to Kubicek's bakery on Atwood Avenue where I often ran, with my dog, Suzy, for a loaf of freshly baked white bread for lunch or sweets to serve later with supper.

Chocolate doughnuts with glossy-chocolate frosting were four cents each at Kubicek's. For eight cents; you could treat yourself to an eclair stuffed with silky-smooth vanilla custard. There were sugared bismarks, coconut crescent butter rolls, and a myriad of other baked goods that peered back at me through the glass showcases, but my favorites were small, heavy dark gingerbread cakes shaped like copper tubs. Studded with nuts and dark raisins, the cakes were coated with chocolate glaze. The very sight and flavor had stayed with me forever. If I was to search for long recipes for my readers, perhaps they could fill my lone request for the bakery treat that had secured a niche in my memory.

Response to the first column was overwhelming. I received a nice letter from a daughter of Mr. Kubicek. A letter from Mrs. Ellestad, a former Talmadge St. resident, identified the gingerbread cakes as "chop suey's". Enclosed in the envelope was a photograph taken in the mid-1940s of a group of us kids in their driveway, taking a break from a neighborhood street parade. Others who once lived in the area confessed that while reading the column they had followed me with their own memories as I ran, "up Talmadge, across St. Paul, down the hill, across the tracks, up the hill, past the fence, through the lot, between the church and rectory, across Atwood Avenue, past Art's Grocery Store to the bakery, where treat dreams were made or were baked early each morning, then displayed in the showcases at eye-level, a height perfect for a little girl with a giant sweet tooth."

To reflect on the past seemed comforting to readers. It came as a form of nourishment in reminding them of when life held special ingredients. Interjecting the good times and reminiscences with descriptions, flavors and recipes became an overnight blue ribbon winner. As innocent as childhood was, so was the simplicity and freshness that launched Cooks' Exchange. It never occurred to me during the early months of writing the column that a cookbook would someday be published. Two-hundred and sixteen weeks later, here it is. . . a wealth of nostalgia stirred in with many of the recipes you requested. They are your favorites -the ones you remember as children, as well as those proudly served at school potlucks, church bazaars, family gatherings, holiday celebrations, local restaurants and down the road to other eating establishments in Wisconsin.

These are the recipes you remembered when vacationing in other states, other islands and other countries. They are the special touches served at your neighbor's kitchen table or a best friend's dining room. . . the ones passed on through the years as well as those introduced as recently as last month. They exude personal touches and personal tastes, beckoning repeat performances for others sometime in the future. It is the past, present and future mixed in with memories that seasoned life for me, for you and others who can identify with a time, a place, an age and an era. The combination is absolutely. . . delicious.

To my parents, Mike and Mary Tripalin, who filled the picnic basket with plenty of love.

Olbrich Park toboggan slide –1947.

Erasing winter's chill

·   •

IF YOU NEVER SPENT AN EVENING TOBOGGANING AT
OLBRICH PARK IN JANUARY WHEN THE
TEMPERATURE WAS WELL BELOW ZERO AND THE
WIND WHIPPED UP CHILL FACTORS OFF LAKE
MONONA, YOU DON'T KNOW WHAT YOU MISSED.
Tobogganing within thick blocks of ice the width of a standard
toboggan, and side ice curbs to prevent straying off course and into
people or trees, brought screams of laughter and nightmarish
pleasures Southerners would never understand. Toboggan slides
were one of the joys of many Madison winters that ended after an
episode of unseasonal February thaws.

Our toboggan was an eight-seater with a khaki-colored canvas
cushion, padded just enough to prevent tailbone crush when we hit
the ice from an airborne position. It was daring and exciting and
required a warm snowsuit, boots, heavy mittens, a wool cap and a
scarf that wrapped around the face to allow just a squint of sight
and nothing more. It also required double joints, or something
pretty close, to achieve what you might call leg-wrapping. My
father always opted for the front seat to protect the rest of us from
frostbite. That meant he would climb the ladder first to reach the
top of the toboggan slide, pulling the sled on a snowy flatbed
adjacent to the steep stairs to the roofless room at the top. Two
park employees waiting for the next thrill-seekers would place the
toboggan high on the wooden platform, then help each one of us
take our positions. The person in front crossed his or her legs,
tucking feet under the curl of the toboggan. The next person sat
snugly behind, wrapping his or her legs over the front rider's legs,
and so on. Once we were in place, looking like some kind of
seasonal insect, we'd hang on tightly as the back of the platform

was lifted to send the toboggan, and us, through the air and downward to the icy path that sent us merrily on our way. The further we went, the longer the trek back up to Oakridge Avenue, but before we knew it we were back on the toboggan platform ready for another flight through winter. Bitter cold and tobogganing always meant cocoa when we arrived home, or chili and cocoa if it was a tobogganing party. Sipping on cocoa was like the calm after a storm and necessary to thaw us out before bedtime. Bitter cold is conducive to baking, too, and spending the day making bread seemed to poke fun at the thermometer that hung by the window near the sink. I never paid much attention to the preparation of homemade bread, but I did know that bread hot from the oven didn't rest on a rack to cool in our house. As soon as it was removed from the oven, it was thickly sliced, then drizzled with olive oil and seasoned with a sprinkling of salt and pepper. It was a perfect accompaniment to a bowl of soup or chowder and a nostalgic reminder of how bread was eaten in the Old Country.

BEEF STOCK

A reader asked if I could find a recipe for beef stock made by roasting meat bones and vegetables in the oven before placing them in a kettle of water. In local author Margaret Guthrie's 1988 cookbook, Best Recipes of Ohio Inns and Restaurants, a baked beef stock was featured from Lock 24 Restaurant in Elkton, Ohio.

3 pounds beef, veal bones
1 large onion quartered, skin on
2 carrots, cut in large chunks
2 celery stalks, with leaves
2 Tablespoons fresh thyme
1 bay leaf
2 Tablespoons tomato paste
4 sprigs parsley, stems only
6 cups water

Place bones, onion, carrots, celery, bay leaf and thyme in a large shallow roasting pan. Bake in a 450-degree oven for about 45 minutes or until the bones are well-browned, turning occasionally. Place in a large stock pot all browned ingredients. Add parsley, tomato paste and water. Bring to a boil. Reduce heat and let stock simmer for 3 to 4 hours, skimming frequently, adding more water as needed. Remove from heat, lift out bones and vegetables with a slotted spoon. Strain the stock through a sieve. Skim off fat with spoon or chill the stock and lift off the solidified fat.

Makes about 5 cups.

Note: This stock can be frozen and kept in the freezer up to 3 months.

Country Kitchen's
Calico Bean Soup

The first soup, initially requested by Pat Smith, Stoughton, was featured in my column after the brunt of a long Wisconsin winter. Yet a tasty kettle of soup is always a gift for all seasons and I was delighted that Country Kitchen International in Minneapolis would share the recipe. However, there are a few readers who have questioned the small amount of beans used. The amounts were further reconfirmed by Country Kitchen's home economists. I say, experiment with more, if you wish, but be careful with additions.

1/2 ounce each of the following dry beans: great northern, butter, red kidney, navy and pinto
1/2 ounce split peas
1 1/2 quarts water
1 1/2 Tablespoons margarine
3/4 cup chopped celery
1/2 cup diced onion
3/4 cup diced ham, preferably dry-cure
1/8 teaspoon garlic powder
1/8 teaspoon pepper
1/2 quart canned diced tomatoes
1/8 teaspoon liquid smoke
1/2 teaspoon lemon juice
1/2 Tablespoon ham base

Carefully remove any small stones from beans and split peas, then rinse in colander and drain well. Place beans in heavy stockpot. Add 1 1/2 quarts of cold water and bring to boil. Remove from heat, cover and let stand for two hours. In another stockpot, melt margarine and saute celery, onion and ham until soft. Add garlic powder, pepper, tomatoes, liquid smoke and lemon juice. Bring to simmer, then add soaked beans plus 8 cups of water beans soaked in. Bring to boil, stirring constantly. Reduce to simmer and add ham base. Cook for two hours, stirring occasionally.

Yield: about 10 servings.

Wisconsin Cheddary Beer Soup

As Wisconsin as it gets, this seasonal soup is a favorite from the Howe family of Howe Plumbing in Madison.

4 Tablespoons butter

1/3 cup chopped green onion

One 8-ounce package shredded cabbage

1/4 cup flour

Two 10 1/2-ounce cans of chicken broth

1/2 cup beer

1 tablespoon Dijon mustard

2 cups half and half, heated

2 cups Cheddar cheese, shredded (about 8 ounces)

Melt butter in large pan. Add onion and cabbage. Cook and stir until vegetables become translucent. Stir in flour and cook one minute. Add broth and beer and mustard. Cover and simmer 30 minutes. Add warm half and half and cheese. Warm gently until heated and cheese melts. Stir to prevent scorching.

Black Bean Soup

I first learned about black beans when living in Key West in the late 1950s. Black beans with rice was a staple of Cuban families and native residents and a mouthwatering aroma drifted through the island's quaint streets and alleys each night around suppertime. This recipe came from a caterer in New York City and was featured in Phyllis Meras' book, "The New Carry-Out Cuisine."

1 pound black beans
3 Tablespoons olive oil
1 Tablespoon minced garlic
3/4 pound Spanish onions, diced
4 stalks celery, diced
6 1/2 cups chicken stock or water
1 ham bone
1 bay leaf
1/2 sweet red pepper, diced
1 Tablespoon ground cumin
1/2 teaspoon cayenne pepper
Salt and pepper, to taste
1 Tablespoon brown sugar
1 Tablespoon lemon juice
1/3 cup sherry
4 Tablespoons chopped fresh parsley
1/2 cup sour cream
1/4 cup chopped scallions
1 hard-boiled egg; chopped, for garnish.

Soak black beans overnight and drain. In a soup pot, heat the olive oil and saute garlic, onions and celery until vegetables are transparent. Add the stock or water, the ham bone, the beans and bay leaf and simmer for 1 hour. Add the red pepper, cumin, cayenne, salt, pepper, brown sugar, lemon juice and sherry and simmer for 20 minutes. Remove ham bone. Puree about a quarter of the soup and mix it back in. If desired, chop the meat from the ham bone and add to soup. Add chopped parsley. Serve soup hot, garnished with a dollop of sour cream and a sprinkling of scallions and chopped egg. Serves 8 to 10.

Sweet and Sour Cabbage Borscht

On an average of once a month I receive a request for the sweet and sour cabbage soup prepared and served in a State Street restaurant. Students and shoppers have been enjoying it for years, but the management is not ready to share the receipe. Pat Morgan, Madison, spent many hours in her own kitchen trying to perfect a soup with similar flavors. She was more than happy to offer her own recipe in response to a reader's request.

2 pounds beef chuck or short ribs
2 quarts water
2 pounds cabbage, shredded
12 prunes
Juice of 2 lemons
3/4 cup brown sugar
1 (1-pound, 13-ounce) can tomatoes
2 apples, grated
1 onion, grated
1 teaspoon salt
1/4 teaspoon pepper

Cover beef with water and simmer for 1 hour. Cool and skim off fat. Add remaining ingredients and simmer 1 hour longer, or until meat is tender. Add more lemon juice or brown sugar to reach desired flavor, or use sour salt in place of lemon.

Serves 8 to 10.

Note: Morgan uses bottled ReaLemon juice, and 1 quart of home canned tomatoes when available.

CHILI CHEESE SOUP

N.W. Chase wondered if I could supply a vegetarian chili recipe from a local catering business. Since the recipe is not available to anyone but the employees, this took its place. Found in the "New Vegetarian Cuisine" by Linda Rosenweig, the soup has added appeal with a touch of old Mexico flavors.

1 Tablespoon margarine
1 cup chopped sweet red peppers
2 Tablespoons chopped canned green peppers (wear plastic gloves when handling)
2 Tablespoons unbleached flour
1 1/2 Tablespoons cornstarch
1 cup water
4 1/2 cups low-sodium vegetable stock
1 cup evaporated skim milk
1 cup drained canned corn
1 medium tomato, seeded and diced
1/2 teaspoon chili powder
1/4 teaspoon ground cumin
1 cup shredded low-fat Cheddar cheese
1/2 teaspoon low-sodium Worcestershire sauce

In a medium no-stick frying pan over medium heat, melt the margarine. Add red peppers and chili peppers; cook, stirring frequently, for 3 to 4 minutes, or until peppers are tender. Set aside. In a small bowl, whisk together the flour and cornstarch. Gradually add water and whisk until smooth. Set aside. In a 3-quart saucepan over medium-high heat, bring stock to a boil. Whisk in flour mixture and milk. Bring back to a boil, whisking constantly. Reduce heat to medium-low. Add corn, tomatoes, chili powder, cumin and peppers. Simmer for 5 to 10 minutes to blend flavors. Stir in the Cheddar and Worcestershire sauce; cook, stirring constantly, until Cheddar has melted.

Serves 4.

Note: If you are making this soup ahead, wait until you reheat it to add the cheese. Can be served with tortilla chips to accompany a Mexican meal, or as a light meal by itself.

Reuben Chowder– Cambridge Country Inn and Pub

Just a 20-minute drive from Madison will open many gift and food treasures within two blocks in Cambridge. This hearty chowder is served with an "old town" touch in an exciting new restaurant of historical value.

1/2 pound butter
1/2 pound sifted all-purpose flour
1 pound celery, diced
1 cup carrots, diced
1 cup yellow onions, diced
8 cups water
3 ounces chicken stock
1/2 cup pickle relish
3/4 pound cooked corned beef brisket, cubed in 1/4 inch pieces
3/4 pound fresh sauerkraut, drained
1 quart 2% milk
1 cup half and half
1 teaspoon Morton's Natures Seasoning Non-Salt
A dash of garlic powder
Rye croutons and shredded Swiss cheese for garnish (optional)

Make a roux over low heat with butter and flour. In a 6-quart stock pot, combine celery, carrots, onions, water, stock, relish, meat, sauerkraut and seasonings. Bring ingredients to a boil; reduce heat and cook until carrots are tender. Add milk and half and half. Increase heat to 150 degrees and slowly blend in roux with wire whip until smooth. Do not overthicken, as the chowder will continue to thicken as it cooks. Serve in individual bowls and garnish with croutons and a sprinkle of shredded Swiss Cheese.

KICKS' SEAFOOD CHOWDER

Kicks closed their restaurant on Whitney Way restaurant, but left us with this delicious memento.

1 cup celery, chopped
1 cup onions, chopped
1/2 cup carrots, chopped
2 cups potato, cubed with skin on
2 Tablespoons chopped garlic
3 Tablespoons dried basil
2 teaspoons salt
1 teaspoon black pepper
3 Tablespoons margarine, divided
Two 28-ounce cans chopped tomatoes
One 24-ounce can tomato juice
3 cups water
One 8-ounce jar clam juice
1/4 cup green pepper, chopped
1 cup zucchini, quartered and sliced
1/2 cup sweet vermouth
8 ounces cooked baby shrimp
8 ounces imitation crab meat

Saute celery, onions, carrots, potato, garlic, basil, salt and pepper in a soup pot with 2 tablespoons margarine until slightly tender. Add chopped tomatoes, tomato juice, water and clam juice, stir, simmer for 45 minutes. While that is simmering, combine green pepper and zucchini in a separate saute pan with 1 tablespoon margarine. Saute until glazed. Remove from heat and add sweet vermouth. Use caution, as it may flame up slightly. Place pan over heat again and reduce vermouth by half. Add this to bulk of soup. Add the baby shrimp and crab meat and bring to a full simmer. Serve hot with oyster crackers. You may add more of any cooked seafood you like to make this chowder even heartier.

Makes approximately one gallon.

Brennan's Onion Soup
Au Gratin

Pat Forseth asked for the "perfect" recipe for baked onion soup. The local country club that served what she had in mind wouldn't respond to my plea, so instead I offered cookbook author and magazine editor Arthur Hettich's own favorite from the French Quarter in New Orleans.

8 Tablespoons butter
1 1/2 cups thinly sliced white onions
1/2 cup all-purpose flour
2 cans (13 3/4 ounces each) beef broth
1 1/2 teaspoons salt
Dash of cayenne
1 egg yolk
2 Tablespoons light cream
4 thin slices French bread
1/2 cup freshly grated Parmesan cheese

Melt butter in a large, heavy saucepan. Saute onions in butter until very soft. Blend in flour and cook for 5 minutes, stirring constantly. Stir in broth, salt and cayenne. Heat to boiling, stirring constantly. Lower heat; simmer for 15 minutes. Beat egg yolk and cream in a small bowl; blend in about 1 cup of the hot soup, then return mixture into saucepan. Ladle soup into 4 individual heatproof bowls. Float a slice of French bread on each and top with Parmesan cheese. Broil, watching carefully, 4 inches from heat, just until cheese turns golden.

Yield: 4 servings.

BAKED POTATO SOUP
THE MACHINE SHED

It is well worth the drive to Rockford, Ill. to stop by for a heartland concept that has won the hearts of Midwesterners as well as travelers from other parts of the country. The "Shed" staff was most accommodating when I arrived to gather information for my article and to sample the soup Anna Zettle, Monroe, and countless others rave about.

2 1/2 pounds baby red potatoes, quartered
1/2 pound raw bacon, diced
1 jumbo yellow onion, diced
1/4 bunch celery, diced
1 quart water
2 ounces chicken base
1 quart milk
1 teaspoon salt
1 teaspoon black pepper
1 1/2 sticks margarine
6 ounces flour
1 cup whipped cream
1/4 bunch parsley, chopped
GARNISH:
Shredded colby cheese, fried bacon bits and chopped green onions.

Boil potatoes in water for 10 minutes. Drain and set aside. In large, heavy pot, saute bacon, onion and celery over medium-high heat until celery is tender. Drain bacon grease and return bacon, onions and celery to pot. Add milk, water, chicken base, salt and pepper. Heat over medium-high heat until very hot. Do not boil. In a heavy, large saucepan, melt margarine and add flour to make a roux. Mix well and allow to bubble, stirring for 1 minute. While constantly stirring soup, add roux slowly. Continue stirring soup until thick and creamy. Stir in potatoes, parsley and cream. Serve while hot. Garnish with shredded colby cheese, fried bacon bits and chopped green onions. Serves 12.

Old-Fashioned Beef and Vegetable Soup

Robert Smith was searching for a hearty vegetable soup like what he remembered from his childhood. "Hollyhocks and Radishes," a cookbook written by award-winning author Bonnie Stewart Mickelson, featured this recipe and what I thought would be a close second.

3 pounds lean short ribs or meaty beef chuck bones
4 onions, coarsely chopped
4 to 6 cups cold water
1 small head cabbage, cut up
3 stalks celery, chopped
8 carrots, diced
One 16-ounce can tomatoes, or tomato bits
One 10 1/2-ounce can tomato soup
1 bay leaf
1 Tablespoon Worcestershire sauce
1 Tablespoon sugar
4 medium potatoes, cut up (optional)
One 10-ounce package frozen peas
One 10-ounce package frozen lima beans
Salt and freshly ground pepper to taste

Place meat and onions in large pot or soup kettle. Add cold water to cover; about 6 cups if you will be adding potatoes, 4 cups otherwise. Cover and bring to a boil, then immediately reduce heat to barely simmer. Cook slowly for 2 hours. Remove meat, and skim fat. Add remaining ingredients to pot except potatoes, peas and beans. Cover and cook slowly another hour. Trim meat of all fat and bone. Return to pot along with potatoes and cook 15 minutes. Add peas and beans; simmer another 10 minutes. Season to taste with salt and freshly ground pepper. Freezes well.

Serves 8-12.

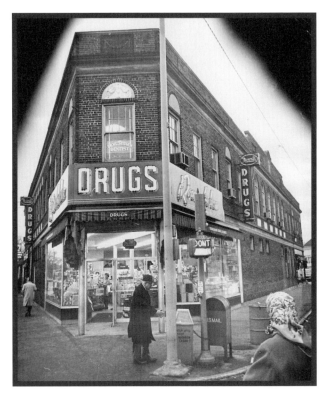

Rennebohm's Drugstore on Atwood Avenue.

Famous
People,
Famous
Places

. . . . •

LOUELLA MORTENSON'S NAME BECAME A HOUSEHOLD WORD WHEN I WAS YOUNG. THIS GRAND LADY OF MADISON AIRWAVES KEPT MOTHERS COMPANY AS THEY IRONED, MENDED AND PREPARED WHOLESOME MEALS FOR THEIR FAMILIES. With a personal touch, she added a special ingredient to the homemaking profession and as one radio listener said, "When Louella Mortenson gives a recipe on the radio, it seems so real I sometimes think I see a bit of flour on her nose."

Listening to the radio back then often took the drudgery out of housework. Tuning in to "Louella" added glamour to the apron and housedress as she turned "monotonous household jobs" into "creative efforts." She stressed the importance of nutrition, good food habits for children, solid family relationships, short cuts in food preparation, and what was new in the world of modern appliances. She shared tips with a pinch of philosophy. To identify with ordinary families, for example, she shared her own simple practice of popping corn with the family every Sunday evening. It was obvious she loved her job as a radio commentator because she became everyone's friend. Mortenson's first radio broadcast was performed in Kansas in 1924. Introduced to Madison in 1928 as a UW Home Economics Extension Agent, she was frequently heard

25

• on WHA Radio. In 1949, she joined the crew at WKOW, and in August 1953, walked into our homes for the first time on WKOW-TV's Channel 27. Almost magically, we witnessed on the screen her charming ways and friendly smile, thus reinforcing our radio friendships of the past. Serving as WKOW's Woman's Program Director from 1949 to 1969, Mortenson often shared the stage with two other television personalities, Blake Kellogg and John Schermerhorn. Together, they savored the sweetness of pioneering local television, as well as the flavors that took grand prizes in annual local and statewide cooking competitions. I was young when television first came to Madison. Recipes, cooking awards, and women's programs were not a part of my daily viewing. It wasn't until later that I would fully appreciate Louella Mortenson as a person, broadcaster, lecturer, writer and food consultant. She received countless awards and deserving recognition on local, state, national and international levels. Mortenson passed away in 1984 at 86. If she were with us today, she would be pleased to know that she is still remembered with great fondness by long-time Madisonians. And be just as happy that we are still using the recipes she shared on a daily, weekly and seasonal basis, like the black walnut cookies requested by Mrs. C.A. Moore, Shullsburg. If you don't have a black walnut tree in your back yard or in a nearby field, check at the Farmers Market.

Regular walnuts could be used, however the distinct black walnut flavor would be missing.

LOUELLA MORTENSON'S
BLACK WALNUT TREATS

1/2 cup butter
1 cup light brown sugar
1 egg
1 teaspoon vanilla
1 1/2 cups all-purpose flour
1/2 teaspoon baking soda
1/2 teaspoon salt
1/2 cup chopped black walnuts

Cream butter. Gradually add sugar. Continue creaming until light and fluffy. Add egg and vanilla. Beat well. Mix flour, soda and salt together. Add to creamed mixture. Add walnuts. Drop from teaspoon onto greased cookie sheets. Bake at 375 degrees about 10 minutes.

Makes about 5 dozen 2-inch cookies.

Louella Mortenson's Sour Cream Oatmeal Cookies

"A cookie-jar favorite"

1 cup butter
2 cups brown sugar, firmly packed
2 eggs
2 1/2 cups flour
1/2 teaspoon salt
1 teaspoon cinnamon
1/2 teaspoon nutmeg
1/4 teaspoon cloves
1 teaspoon soda
1 cup sour cream
2 cups oatmeal
2 cups raisins and/or dates
1 cup nutmeats, chopped, (optional)

Cream butter and sugar; add eggs and beat. Add sifted dry ingredients and sour cream alternately. Mix in oatmeal, fruit, and nuts, if desired. Drop on greased pan and bake at 425 degrees until golden brown, about 15 minutes, depending on size of cookie. Do not overbake.

Louella Mortenson's Frosted Prune Bars

"Easy, economical, wonderful flavor"

1 pound uncooked pitted prunes, cut in pieces
1 cup boiling water
3 eggs
1/2 cup salad oil
2 cups flour
1 1/2 cups sugar
1 teaspoon salt
1 1/4 teaspoon baking soda
1 teaspoon cinnamon
1/2 teaspoon nutmeg
1/4 teaspoon ginger
1/2 cup chopped nutmeats

Pour boiling water over prune pieces. Cool. Beat eggs until very light. Add oil and beat thoroughly. Fold in sifted dry ingredients. Add prunes (with water) and nuts. Pour into greased cake roll pan 15 1/2x10 1/2x1-inch. Bake at 350 degrees for 35 minutes. Cool. Spread with icing. Cut into bars.

Another Walgreen's drugstore opened in Madison last week. Massive and modern, the building is nothing less than imposing, with a seemingly endless inventory of necessities that becomes overwhelming even to today's young customers. Humble little corner drugstores are becoming as rare as humble little corner grocery stores. It is a safe bet that Governor Rennebohm, who served the state from 1948 to 1950 and founded Rennebohm Drug Stores, would be in awe of it all. Yet something remains missing for which we old-time Madisonians cannot find a cure. The "affliction" revolves around the lack of Rennebohm Drug Store's soda fountains, lunch counters and booths, where many of us spent fragments of our lives.

In 1950, when I had just embraced teenagehood, there were already 13 Rennebohm's in Madison. Tall marble counters with spin-around stools were as important to the stores as a bottle of aspirin and a box of Kleenex. For a break from the heat of summer you could stop in for a cool chocolate soda layered in a tall fluted glass, or a thick malted milk whirred to perfection in a deep stainless steel container. If you didn't have a quarter and still wanted something special to sip, a squirt or two of strawberry sauce from a levered receptacle suddenly made a plain Coke spectacular. Lime Coke? Just say the word and your Coke took on a slight green hue. Cherry Cokes were a giant step above Dr. Pepper and happened to be my favorite. If snow was falling and you just missed the bus home, you could rest your feet and warm your fingers while treating yourself to a pre-supper piece of cherry pie with coffee. When time was of the essence during the noon hour, ham salad or egg salad on white bread, a green olive-nut sandwich, beef barbecue on a bun, a grilled "Bucky" burger (double decker with a thin bun in between), or a bowl of chicken noodle soup could be served within minutes. Meeting friends before going to the LOFT (Lots of Fun Times) on East Doty Street became even better when Hot Fudge Mary Jane's and warm grilled danishes were served to people-packed booths.

Forget the Rennebohm legend? Impossible.

Rennebohm's Bran Muffins

10 ounces margarine (2 1/2 sticks)
1 3/4 cups granulated sugar
2 teaspoons salt
5 eggs
2 1/2 cups unbleached white flour
1 1/2 cup whole wheat flour
3 1/4 cups whole bran
3 teaspoons baking powder
1 teaspoon baking soda
1/4 cup powdered milk
1/2 cup water
Preheat oven to 400 degrees

In large bowl, cream margarine, sugar and salt with electric mixer. Add eggs and continue to cream until mixture is smooth. Combine white flour, whole what flour, bran, baking powder, baking soda and powdered milk. Beat water into the batter, then add the combined dry ingredients in three parts, mixing well after each addition. Beat for 2 minutes. Completely fill well-greased or paper lined muffin tins and bake for 25 minutes, or until center of muffins bounce back when touched.

Makes 2 dozen.

Rennebohm's Brownies

When Madisonian Dorothy Jones went to work at Rennebohm's Commissary in 1930, this was the brownie baked in the commissary for their various locations in town. She also remembers a letter and poem that had been written and delivered on election night in 1947 when Oscar Rennebohm was elected Governor of Wisconsin. The auther suggested that it be sung to the tune of "O Tannenbaum" O Rennebohm. O Rennebohm We love your brownies a la mode. Others may call you "The Pharm" But to me, you'll always be O Rennebohm, O Rennebohm O's for Oscar Rennebohm!

1 1/2 cups sugar

1/2 cup butter

3 eggs

3 squares unsweetened baking chocolate, melted

3/4 cup flour

1/2 teaspoon baking powder

Pinch of salt

1 teaspoon vanilla

1 cup nut meats, chopped

Cream together sugar and butter. Beat in eggs, one at a time, mixing well. Add melted baking chocolate.

Mix together dry ingredients and add to batter. Stir in vanilla and fold in nuts. Batter will be very stiff. Grease and flour 9x12-inch pan. Bake at 300 to 325 degrees for 25 to 30 minutes. Use your oven as your baking guide.

Note: For a Rennebohm Hot Fudge Mary Jane, top a brownie with a scoop of vanilla ice cream and drizzle with hot fudge.

Rennebohm's Chicken Noodle Soup

4 quarts of homemade chicken stock, or 3 quarts canned chicken broth with 1 quart of water

2 1/2 cups diced carrots

2 cups diced celery

1 1/3 cups diced onions

1 1/2 cups diced chicken

1 1/2 pound frozen noodles

Place all ingredients except the noodles in a large stockpot and bring to a boil. Add noodles and simmer for 45 minutes or until noodles are tender.

RENNEBOHM'S HOT FUDGE MARY JANE BROWNIES

5 1/2 ounces semisweet chocolate
2 sticks plus 2 tablespoons margarine
3 cups sugar
4 eggs
2 cups flour
3/4 teaspoons baking powder
1/4 teaspoon salt
1/2 teaspoon vanilla
3/4 cup walnuts, coarsely chopped

Preheat oven to 375 degrees. Melt chocolate and margarine in small saucepan and set aside. In large mixing bowl, cream sugar and eggs together with an electric mixer, then incorporate well. In separate bowl, combine flour, baking powder and salt. Add dry ingredients by spoonfuls to chocolate mixture, beating well after each addition. Add vanilla, combine well and stir in walnuts. Pour into well-greased 9x12-inch pan and bake for 25 to 30 minutes. Brownies should be moist and chewy.

Makes 2 dozen.

Note: For a Hot Fudge Mary Jane, top a brownie with a scoop of vanilla ice cream and drizzle with warmed hot fudge sauce. Top with a dollop of whipped cream.

Rennebohm's Cherry Pie

4 cups pitted cherries
1/2 cup sugar
2 Tablespoons powdered, unflavored gelatin
9-inch unbaked pie shell

Preheat oven to 425 degrees. In a large bowl, sprinkle sugar over cherries and let stand overnight. Drain well the next morning, reserving the juice and adding enough water to make 1 2/3 cups. In small saucepan, bring the juice to a boil and add gelatin. Cook until thick and clear.

Pour over cherries and stir to coat fruit with the glaze. Pour into pie shell and bake for 15 minutes, then reduce heat to 375 degrees and bake 25 to 30 minutes longer until crust is golden brown.

Rennebohm's Classic Pecan Pie

3 eggs, slightly beaten
1 cup Karo, light or dark
1 cup sugar
2 Tablespoons margarine; melted
1 teaspoon vanilla
1 1/2 cups pecans
1 unbaked 9-inch pie crust

In large bowl, combine first five ingredients until well blended. Stir in pecans. Pour into pie crust. Bake at 350 degrees for 50 to 55 minutes, or until knife inserted halfway between center and edge comes clean.

Serves 8.

RENNEBOHM'S BANANA CAKE

1 1/2 cup sugar
1/2 cup butter
2 eggs, well beaten
5 Tablespoons sour milk
1 teaspoon baking soda
1 3/4 cups flour
1 cup mashed bananas

Cream together sugar and butter. Add well-beaten eggs. Mix together sour milk and baking soda and add to batter. Add flour, then mashed bananas. Preheat oven and bake in 2 greased and floured layer pans, or a 9x12-inch pan, at 325 to 350 degrees, for 25 to 30 minutes or until done, using your oven as your baking guide. If layers are baked, cool on rack and put together with filling of your choice, then frost.

Longtime Madisonians remember Carson Gulley as a congenial man who proudly wore the tall, white hat of his profession as a chef of unequaled parallel.

Actually, the term "chef" fails to fully define the man who studied the importance of food under the watchful eye of George Washington Carver at the Tuskegee Institute; directed training for Navy cooks and bakers during World War II; received the 1948 Award of Merit from the Wisconsin Restaurant Association; is listed in the 1950 edition of "Who's Who in Colored America"; wrote two cookbooks and served as host of a weekly television program, "What's Cookin"; and as host of the WIBA Cooking School of the Air; owned a restaurant and catering business with his wife, Beatrice; served as senior chef with the UW-Madison Division of Residence Halls for 27 years; had a campus building named in his honor (Carson Gulley Commons); acted as judge for the second Wisconsin State Journal recipe contest in the 1940s . . . and that just skims the surface. Yet with all the titles and accolades to his credit, countless thousands remember Gulley best for his Fudge Bottom Pie. It was to be one of his many legacies to food enthusiasts in Madison.

Carson Gulley was born in Arkansas in 1897. At age 25, he left sharecropping to become a restaurant dishwasher. Little did he realize the day the cook quit that the step he was forced to take on a moment's notice from the sink to the cutting board would capture his heart for the rest of his life.

Stepping stones for advancement occurred in well-known restaurants, hotels, and resorts throughout the United States until a path led to Madison, where Gulley would remain until his death in 1962. I was not surprised when a reader requested Gulley's Fudge Bottom Pie recipe. I remember consuming slices of the slippery smooth tasting masterpiece at the Memorial Union as a UW-Madison student, and while savoring a facsimile at the Simon House restaurant on South Butler Street. It never mattered how full you were after dining because there was always enough room left for that particular dessert.

For all of Madison and its students, past and present, who have enjoyed Gulley's famous pie for breakfast, lunch, dinner and any time in between, here is a flavor you will never forget. Carson Gulley would be pleased to know that his recipe once again is being shared with those who remember, and with those who never had the joy of tasting his Fudge Bottom Pie . . . until now.

Memorial Union
Fudge Bottom Pie

Anyone who missed out in not having more than one slice of this, also missed out on one of the great pleasures of being a UW Madison student.

1 1/2 cups graham cracker crumbs
2 Tablespoons powdered sugar
1/4 teaspoon salt
6 Tablespoons butter
3 ounces bitter chocolate
1/4 cup sugar
1/4 cup water
1/2 cup sugar
1/4 cup cornstarch
1/4 teaspoon salt
2 cups milk
3 egg yolks, slightly beaten
1 teaspoon vanilla
Whipped cream, sweetened, if desired
Shaved bitter chocolate for garnish.

For crust, combine graham cracker crumbs with powdered sugar and salt. Melt butter, pour into crumb mixture and combine. Press into a 9-inch pie pan and bake at 375 degrees for 5 to 10 minutes. Melt bitter chocolate. Combine 1/4 cup sugar and water and bring to a boil. Add to melted chocolate and beat well. Spread evenly over bottom of pie shell. In a saucepan, combine 1/2 cup sugar, cornstarch and salt and gradually stir in milk. Place over medium heat and cook, stirring constantly, until mixture boils and thickens. Cook two minutes longer, then remove from heat. Stir a small amount of hot mixture into slightly beaten egg yolks, then stir into hot mixture slowly. Return to medium heat and cook another 2 minutes, stirring constantly. Remove from stove and stir in vanilla. Cool to room temperature, then pour into pie shell. Cover with whipped cream and garnish, if desired, with shaved bitter chocolate.

CARSON GULLEY'S FUDGE BOTTOM PIE

From "Seasoning Secrets and Favorite Recipes of Carson Gulley," ©1956

CRUST:

1 cup graham cracker crumbs

1/4 cup powdered sugar

1/3 cup melted butter

Mix ingredients, press into pie tin and bake 5 minutes at 350 degrees.

FILLING:

2 cups milk

1 cup sugar

2 Tablespoons cornstarch

4 eggs, separated, 1 Tablespoon gelatin, softened in 1/4 cup cold water

1 1/4 ounces baking chocolate

1/4 teaspoon cream of tartar

TOPPING:

Whipped cream.

Grated sweet chocolate

Heat milk in a double boiler. Blend cornstarch and half of the sugar together. Add enough of the hot milk to moisten well, then add to the balance of the hot milk and continue cooking in double boiler. Beat egg yolks, pour some of the hot milk mixture over them, beating well, and then add them to the hot milk mixture in the double boiler. Cook, stirring constantly until thick and smooth. Add softened gelatin, blend well and set mixture aside to cool. Melt chocolate over hot water. Take 1 cup of the hot custard mixture, stir it into the melted chocolate and set aside to cool. After the custard has cooled, but not become stiff, beat the egg whites with the cream of tartar. When eggs are stiff enough to hold peaks, add the remaining 1/2 cup of sugar gradually and continue beating until well blended. Fold beaten egg whites into the cooled vanilla custard mixture. Pour the cooled chocolate custard mixture into baked graham cracker pie shell.

Pour the custard, egg white mixture over it, and refrigerate several hours, or overnight. Top with whipped cream and grated sweet chocolate before serving.

Left to right: Duane Grinde, Sonja Sherven, Catherine Tripalin and Tom Whitmore having a late dinner at Matt Lombardino's State Street Italian Village following a 1956 Senior Dance.

Teen years
and lots of fun

. . . . •

THE CARD WAS A PASSPORT TO FUN TIMES . . . LOTS
OF FUN TIMES, MEANING THE LOFT. FROM 1946
TO THE RESTLESSNESS OF THE 1960S THAT CAUSED
ITS DEMISE, THE CLUB IN THE TWO-STORY
BUILDING AT 16 E. DOTY ST. WAS ONE OF THE BEST
THINGS THAT HAPPENED TO A MADISON TEEN-
AGER. A USO in World War II, the place was turned into a
gathering spot for teen-agers and rocked with tunes from the
corner jukebox or local bands on stage.

Under the guidance of the Madison School Board and the city
Recreation Department, director Erin "Ace" Karp created a home-
away-from-home by offering a place to socialize, snack and play
cards for youth who were at least 16 years old or high school
sophomores. Pool, billiard and pingpong tables covered the expanse
of the second floor. Below, a large dance floor was alive with
flickering lights and a mirrored globe suspended from the ceiling.
Here was where the two-step, schottische, polka, bunny hop and
jitterbug were learned and polished. And, for many, here was where
romance began. All of this, plus more, was available for annual
dues of $1 plus the initial cost of 20 cents for an ID card. Ask
anyone to describe his or her LOFT days, and the response would
be the same. It was where the action was. High school athletes were
recognized for their accomplishments each year, just as the annual
jitterbug contest brought scores of couples to twist, turn and jive it
up to "In the Mood" and "Sweet Georgia Brown." (Central
dominated the contest for years — that is, until East took high
honors in 1956 and '57.) If the LOFT was great throughout the
year, it became even better in mid-March during the WIAA Boys
State Basketball tournament. Following evening games at the Field

- House, the LOFT swelled at the seams as visiting teen-agers had a chance to experience what Madison offered its youth population. And, if we had our all-too-familiar mid-March-madness snowstorm that disrupted travel plans, tables were set up at the LOFT to arrange accommodations in area homes for stranded visitors. Of course, girls wanted boys to stay at their homes and boys wanted girls. Those whose parents gave in were envied by others. For $3 a day, an out-of-town teen had a clean bed, a warm meal and another home away from home. For Madison residents who opened their homes to high schoolers during tournament time, the meals prepared there were what we call, with great fondness today, "comfort food." Just plain all-American meals for the visitors or, at times, stranded masses to savor.

CHEESEBURGER CHOWDER

A cheeseburger in a bowl. What teenager wouldn't love to share a kitchen table and a kettle of this with friends?

1 pound ground beef
2 cups potatoes, peeled and cubed
1/2 cup chopped celery
1/2 cup frozen chopped onions
2 Tablespoons chopped green pepper
12 ounces beef broth
Salt, to taste
2 1/2 cups milk
3 Tablespoons all-purpose flour
1 cup sharp Cheddar cheese, shredded

In heavy kettle, brown beef. Drain off excess fat. Stir in potatoes, celery, onion, green pepper, broth and salt. Cover and cook until vegetables are tender. This should take about 20 minutes. Blend 1/2 cup milk with flour. Add to soup in kettle along with remaining milk. Cook and stir until bubbling. Add cheese and heat until cheese melts. Stir frequently.

Makes 6 to 8 cups.

(Recipe from "550 Fabulous Soups," by Susan Hall)

Note: A similar recipe used less meat, excluded potatoes, celery and beef broth, using, instead, an 11-ounce can of Cheddar cheese soup with 1 1/4 cups milk with the addition of 1/8 teaspoon Worcestershire sauce for flavoring. Try experimenting with both recipes.

Secret Ingredient Sloppy Joe

Liquid smoke adds a touch of the outdoors to this simple, economical and tasty treat for a group of teenagers.

1 1/2 pounds lean ground beef
1/2 cup chopped onion
1 Tablespoon prepared mustard
3/4 cup ketchup
2/3 cup water
1/4 cup brown sugar
1/2 teaspoon liquid smoke flavoring

Brown meat and onion over medium heat. Drain well. Add remaining ingredients and stir thoroughly. Simmer uncovered for 10 minutes, stirring occasionally. Spoon onto buns.

Serves 4 to 6.

Texas Chili Dogs

We used to roast weiners on branch sticks over campfires in the woods of Wisconsin. They do things a little different down in Texas by adding beans and chopped tomatoes to a sauce to replace the "traditional" mustard and onions we were raised on.

2 Tablespoons oil
1 large onion, chopped
2 garlic cloves, chopped
1/2 pound lean ground beef
1 (15-ounce) can Italian-style chopped tomatoes, drained
1 (15-ounce) can chili beans
1 Tablespoon chili powder, or to taste
Salt and pepper
Hot dogs
6 hot dog buns
Chopped raw onion, optional

In a skillet, heat the oil, add onion and garlic, and saute for 5 minutes. Add beef and saute until brown. Add tomatoes, beans, chili powder, salt and pepper to taste. Cover and simmer for 10 minutes. Add the hot dogs and simmer for another five minutes to heat them through. Partially fill each hot dog bun with the beef-chili mixture. Place a hot dog on top. Top with additional chopped raw onion, if desired, and serve.

Yield: 6 chili dogs

Hot Dog Sauce

Mary Shampo's northern Italian family collected favorite recipes for a cookbook to pass on to their children and grandchildren. Although not Italian, the flavors in this sauce will bring back good memories for many.

1 1/2 pounds ground beef
1 medium onion, chopped
Salt and pepper to taste
1 Tablespoon dry mustard
2 Tablespoons prepared mustard
1 cup vinegar
2 cups ketchup
1/2 cup sugar
1 cup water
1/2 package of mixed pickling spices (from approximately a 1 1/4-pound package) tied in a sack using cheesecloth or a similar fabric.

Cook meat in fry pan with onions, salt and pepper. Drain if necessary. Add mixture of mustards, vinegar, ketchup, sugar and water with tied sack of mixed spices. Simmer, covered, until well blended. Remove sack. Serve mixture over hot dogs.

Deluxe Hamburgers

Baked burgers for a crowd of 30 could mean the team, the coaches, and even a few cheerleaders. The recipe is from the local YWCA fundraising cookbook of staff and resident favorites.

5 pounds ground beef

3 eggs

1 1/2 cups bread crumbs

1/2 cup (2 ounces) grated Parmesan cheese

1/2 cup relish

1 cup chopped Bermuda onion

1/2 cup ketchup

1/4 cup Worcestershire sauce

1/4 teaspoon salt

1/4 teaspoon black pepper

Vegetable oil

Combine all ingredients, except for oil. Mix thoroughly and shape into 1-inch-thick patties using 1/2-cup measure. Sear each side of patties in oil in skillet, draining excess fat when necessary. Place patties on baking sheet and bake at 350 degrees for 15 to 20 minutes.

Yield: 30 servings.

HOMEMAKER'S CASSEROLE

If you were lucky enough to host out-of-town teen fans at your house during the State High School Basketball tournament time and a blizzard kept them in town for an extra day or two, this would be a sure winner and a taste of home.

1 package of Creamettes
One 10 1/2-ounce can condensed cream-style soup (mushroom, celery)
1 cup milk
1 Tablespoon chopped pimiento
1 Tablespoon chopped green pepper
1 Tablespoon chopped onion
1/2 teaspoon black pepper
1/4 pound processed sharp cheese, grated or cut in cubes
One can tuna

Cook Creamettes according to general directions on package. Combine soup, milk, chopped pimiento, green pepper, onion and pepper. Place over low heat, add grated cheese and stir occasionally, until the cheese is melted. Mix Creamettes and one can of tuna in a 1 1/2-quart casserole. Blend in cheese sauce and refrigerate. When ready to serve, place in oven at 325 degrees about 30 minutes or until sauce is bubbling. May also be baked immediately without refrigeration at 325 degrees for about 15 minutes.

Serves 6.

SPAGHETTI SAUCE

Spaghetti sauce is a snap to prepare. All one needs is a minute now and then to stir the richness of tomato pulp and seasonings that simmer on the back burner. Cooking sauce in a crock pot eliminates the stirring. In fact, this is such a carefree method that once Bill Johnson used his crockpot 16 years ago for spaghetti sauce, he never returned to the oven kettle. It is perfect for a group of friends to enjoy in a warm kitchen on a cold evening after the game.

1 pound lean ground beef
1 large onion, chopped
1 clove garlic, minced
2 (1-pound) cans tomatoes, cut up
One (8-ounce) can tomato sauce
One (12-ounce) can tomato paste
1 cup beef bouillon
2 Tablespoons minced parsley
1 Tablespoon brown sugar
1 teaspoon dried oregano
1 teaspoon dried basil
1 teaspoon salt
1/4 teaspoon pepper

In large skillet or slow-cooking pot with browning unit, crumble meat with onion and garlic. Break up pieces of meat with fork and cook until it loses its red color. Drain excess fat. In slow-cooking pot, combine browned meat, onions and garlic with remaining ingredients. Cover and cook on low for 6 to 8 hours. Serve over hot spaghetti. May be made ahead of time and frozen.

Makes 6 to 8 servings.

Never Fail
Scalloped Potatoes

As a favorite in Mary Sweeney's household, this basic potato recipe will be used over and over again. Add ham, sauteed mushrooms, vegetables for color, or whatever you think will add a special touch. It's just that simple.

5 raw peeled medium-size potatoes, sliced
2 Tablespoons diced onion
6 Tablespoons butter
1 1/2 cups milk
2 Tablespoons cornstarch
Salt and pepper, to taste
1/2 cup shredded Cheddar cheese

Mix potatoes and onion and place in greased 2-quart casserole. Make sauce by combining butter, milk, cornstarch, salt and pepper. Cook until smooth. Add cheese, stirring until well-blended. Pour over potatoes. Bake 90 minutes at 350 degrees, uncovered. Recipe can be doubled.

CAKE DOUGHNUTS

Forty-two years ago, Wonewoc reader Evelyn Fick received a penny postcard from a friend with this recipe written on the back. She has been making them ever since and claims they are fool-proof. They would make a great morning finale after a late night teen slumber party, or for any age group.

4 cups sifted flour
4 teaspoons baking powder
1/2 teaspoon cinnamon
1/2 teaspoon nutmeg
1/2 teaspoon salt
1/3 cup shortening
5 egg yolks
1 cup sugar
1 cup milk

Sift flour, then add dry ingredients. Sift again. Melt shortening. Beat egg yolks until very light and thick. Gradually add sugar, then add melted (cooled) shortening. Gradually add milk, then flour mixture; blend thoroughly. Roll out 1/3-inch thick on floured board and cut with doughnut cutter. Fry a few at a time until done. While warm, roll in additional granulated sugar or powdered sugar.

Makes 24 large doughnuts.

ROOT BEER FLOAT CAKE

Your favorite soda fountain drink as a cake, with frosting that resembles cool billows of foam.

1 package Betty Crocker SuperMoist white cake mix
1 1/4 cups root beer
1/4 cup vegetable oil
2 eggs

Heat oven to 350 degrees. Generously grease and flour rectangular pan, 13x9x2 inches. Beat cake mix (dry), root beer, oil and eggs in large bowl on low speed 30 seconds. Beat on high speed 2 minutes, scraping bowl occasionally. Pour into pan. Bake 30 to 40 minutes or until toothpick inserted in center comes out clean; cool. Frost with Root Beer Cream. Sprinkle with crushed root beer-flavored hard candies if desired.

Serves 16

ROOT BEER CREAM:
1/2 package (2.8-ounce size) whipped topping mix (1 envelope)
1/2 cup chilled root beer

Beat topping mix (dry) and root beer in medium bowl on high speed about 4 minutes or until thickened. Frost.

STRAWBERRY PUNCH

Pretty and delicious, here is a punch that has filled many large cut glass bowls and tiny matching glass cups during Prom parties and sorority teas.

Three (6-ounce) cans frozen lemonade concentrate

One (10-ounce) package frozen strawberries (or 1 1/2 cups fresh strawberries and 1/2 cup sugar)

1 quart chilled ginger ale

Place strawberries, slightly thawed, in blender. Add lemonade and 3 cans of water. Cover and blend. Place in punch bowl or pitcher. Add ginger ale.

Makes 20 (3-ounce) servings.

GRAHAM CRACKER DATE ROLL

Just a little fancier than brownies and Rice Krispie bars. They would have added an elegant touch to sorority teas.

1 pound graham cracker crumbs
1 pound dates, cut into small pieces
1/2 pound marshmallows, cut fine
1 cup finely chopped walnuts
1 cup coffee cream (whipped cream or half and half)
Whipped cream, optional
Maraschino cherries, optional
Reserve 1 cup crumbs.

Mix other ingredients together. Form into a roll and coat in reserved crumbs. Chill in refrigerator overnight in long loaf pan. Slice and serve with whipped cream and a maraschino cherry.

Serves 14 to 16.

Note: Two recipes included additional ingredients, one using a 9-ounce can of undrained crushed pineapple, another calling for grated orange rind.

Kit-Kat Bars

Requested often, this bar took first place honors in its category in the 1989 Wisconsin State Journal cookbook contest for Verona resident Rita Goddard.

2 cups graham cracker crumbs

1 cup margarine

1/3 cup sugar

1 cup brown sugar

1/2 cup milk

25 club crackers

1/2 cup chocolate chips

1/2 cup butterscotch chips

2/3 cup peanut butter

Mix crumbs, margarine, sugars and milk together in pan. Bring to boil; boil 5 minutes, stirring constantly. Put one layer of crackers in an ungreased 9x13-inch pan. Pour half of the boiled mixture on top. Put a second layer of crackers and top with remaining boiled mixture. Top with one more layer of crackers. Melt together the chips and peanut butter. Spread over top of crackers. Cool and cut.

Yield: about 63 pieces.

OATMEAL CRUNCH COOKIES

As requested by Pat Kelly Walkington from the stapled green cookbook we used in the early 1950s in our junior high home economic class at East High school. If I remember correctly, she and Kay Schultz Deminter consumed most of the raw dough before the cookies were baked.

1 cup shortening
1 cup brown sugar
1 cup white sugar
2 well-beaten eggs
1 1/2 cups sifted flour
1 teaspoon soda
1 teaspoon salt
3 cups oatmeal
1 teaspoon vanilla

Cream shortening. (May use 1/2 butter and 1/2 shortening.) Add sugar gradually, first brown, then white. Add eggs. Add sifted flour and soda. Add oatmeal and vanilla. Drop by teaspoonful on greased pan. Spread out each cookie with knife. Bake at 300 degrees for 20 minutes.

Scrumptious Butterscotch Sauce

I remember my teen years as being carefree and fun. Calories were never discussed. As a result, the more ice cream and goopy sauce, the better.

1 tablespoon cornstarch
1 1/4 cups light brown sugar, packed
1/2 cup dairy half and half
2 tablespoons light corn syrup
1/8 teaspoon salt
1/4 cup butter
1 teaspoon vanilla extract

In 1 1/2-quart casserole, stir together cornstarch and brown sugar. Stir in half and half, corn syrup and salt. Add butter. Cover. Microwave at high 3 1/2 to 4 1/2 minutes, stirring after 2 minutes, until thickened and sugar is dissolved. Add vanilla and stir until smooth and well blended. Serve warm or cold.

Makes 1 1/2 cups.

Talmadge Street Melting Pot – about 1947.
Taken in David and Chuckie Ellestad's driveway.

The great melting pot

. . . . •

ONE OF MY GREAT PLEASURES WAS GROWING UP WITH THE McCORMICKS. AN IRISH-CATHOLIC FAMILY WITH NINE KIDS IN A BLUE-COLLAR NEIGHBORHOOD ON THE EAST SIDE WAS LIKE A MILLION COLORFUL SPARKS SNAPPING EVERY WAKING MOMENT OF EVERY DAY. To put it simply, they added unparalleled excitement to Talmadge Street. It is no wonder that each year, when St. Patrick's Day is celebrated, I think of Bob, Bill, George, Tom, Dick, Mike, Patrick, Mary and Ann, and their parents, Robert and Leone, whom we always referred to as Mr. and Mrs. McCormick. A few of the more vocal members of the family used to tease me about not being Irish, and on March 17 they expected me to wear green to pay homage to the saint and to . . . them. The more they reminded me, the more rebellious I became. I was young. How would I know that everyone should wear a wee bit 'o green, whether Irish or not? So, I'd wear red, orange or black, just to make my own statement. They'd be proud of me today, for every March 17 I wear on my lapel a green shamrock to celebrate the day with the best of them. It is my way of paying respect to the folks of Ireland and St. Patrick, while making a connection with the entire McCormick family. Their father, known as "Mack" to most, was a barber by trade, but spent many years involved in politics, ringing doorbells during evening hours for 17th Ward residents to sign seasonal petitions. He was an earthy guy with a great laugh and an Irish zest for living. On March 5, 1995 I attended the funeral of Mrs. McCormick. It was a day of poignant celebration, not only for her 90 years of longevity, her kind and gentle ways, the love she shared with her children, and her accomplishments, but also because of the special place waiting for

• her in heaven. During the course of the day, fond memories were
exchanged with all nine "kids" of the 1930s, 40s, and 50s when we
were growing up together. Interspersed were hugs, tears, laughter
and the realization of how much we truly cared for each other.
Invariably, when reminiscing, food enters the conversation. It
started with recollections of Ole Olson's cream puffs and moved on
to the currants we picked behind Freitag's garage. The crab apples
from the McCormicks' back yard made delicious jelly, and the
snow apples from our tree were perfect for pies, yet, for whatever
reason, we used to swipe apples from Caruso's tree next door to the
McCormicks. Minnie and Arne Ostgoord's mature grape vine
entangled on a fence that ran from the front sidewalk to the garage,
was laden with heavy bunches, rationed between the heavy kettle
and us kids, as well as the spicy little pfeffernusse Minnie made
during the holiday season. And there was Mabel Anderson, lutefisk
and lefse. Soups, stews and sauces seasoned the air with ethnicity
and the memories were soothing, but somehow, before our food
recollections had been completed, we were back in the throes of
being Irish. It had been a melting pot of flavors, but on March 17,
the McCormicks reigned king with . . . corned beef.

BALKENBRIJ

B. Ann Kivett, Montello, recalled "something
wonderful" that a German woman used to prepare during
the Depression. Stirred with a "sawed-off-broom handle,
the mixture was poured from a kettle to set firm in a loaf
pan. After it had properly chilled, it was sliced and fried
in bacon grease, then served with a drizzling of syrup.

2 cups water
1 to 2 teaspoons salt
2 cups fried out cracklings from pork
1 cup buckwheat flour
1 cup white flour

Place salt and cracklings in kettle with water. Boil, then
add remaining ingredients and stir with wooden spoon
until mixture leaves sides of pan. Pack into loaf pan and
chill. Slip out of pan and slice about 1/2-inch thick. Fry
in lard in fry pan until golden brown and crisp. Drizzle
with syrup and eat like a pancake.

Note: Allspice can be added to water for flavor.

CHINESE HOT & SOUR SOUP

My friend, Carl Maglio, spent many hours with me at his kitchen table discussing the Italian food he so loved. But when he and his wife, Rose, dined out, they would visit Chinese restaurants to satisfy his craving for hot and sour soup. Maglio passed away unexpectedly before I had a chance to feature his request, so I offered this in his memory.

6 cups chicken broth
1/3 pound lean pork
3 Tablespoons soy sauce
3 Tablespoons vinegar
1 teaspoon pepper
1 can Chinese vegetables
1 can mushrooms
10 ounces tofu (bean curd)
1 egg, beaten
1 teaspoon cornstarch
1 Tablespoon chopped green onion

Cut pork into 1/4-inch strips. Add to broth after marinating in 1 tablespoon soy sauce. Add seasonings and boil 10 minutes. Add vegetables and cut up tofu and boil 3 minutes. Mix cornstarch with a little cold water and add while stirring. Add egg while stirring, then onion.

Serves 4 to 6.

Hungarian Mushroom Soup

From the Inner Garden Cafe in Napa, Calif., this recipe was offered to Mary Ziegler in our failed attempt to secure a similar one from a local restaurant owner.

2 cups onion, chopped
4 Tablespoons butter
1 pound mushrooms, sliced
2 Tablespoons fresh dill weed, chopped, or 2 teaspoons dry dill
2 cups stock or water
1 Tablespoon soy sauce
1 Tablespoon Hungarian paprika
3 Tablespoons flour
1 cup milk
1 teaspoon salt
Dash of pepper
2 teaspoons fresh lemon juice
3/4 cup sour cream
1/4 cup fresh parsley, chopped

Saute onions in 2 tablespoons butter for 5 to 10 minutes. Add mushrooms, 1 teaspoon dill, 1/2 cup stock or water, soy and paprika. Cover and simmer for 15 minutes. Melt remaining 2 tablespoons butter in separate large saucepan. Whisk in flour, cook a few minutes, whisking constantly. Add milk. Cook, stirring frequently, over low heat until thick (about 10 minutes). Stir in mushroom mixture and remaining stock. Cover and simmer for 10 to 15 minutes. Before serving, add salt, pepper, lemon juice, sour cream and extra dill. Garnish with parsley.

Serves 4.

German Potato Apple Stew

Janet Alwardt's search for the prune soup her elderly Polish uncle remembers his grandmother making many years ago ended up with this honorable mention recipe Linda Karlen submitted for the State Journal's 1984 cookbook. Although its origin is a neighboring country, Pam Valenta hoped it would be similar enough for Karlen's uncle to enjoy equally as well.

2 Tablespoons butter
1 1/2 cups sliced onion
1 Tablespoon flour
1 cup chicken broth
1 cup apple juice
2 Tablespoons lemon juice
1/2 teaspoon salt
1/4 teaspoon caraway seeds
1 1/2 pounds Idaho potatoes, unpeeled and cut into large chunks
1 pound cooked ham, cut in large chunks
1/2 pound pitted prunes; 2 red apples, cored and cut into wedges

In Dutch oven or large, covered saucepan, melt butter; saute onion until golden. Stir in flour and gradually add broth, apple juice, lemon juice, salt and caraway seeds. Stir until slightly thickened. Add potatoes, ham and prunes; bring to a boil. Cover and simmer 15 minutes. Add apples. Cover and simmer an additional 15 to 20 minutes until potatoes and apples are tender; stir occasionally.

Makes 4 servings.

Fettuccine Alfredo

Here it is. . . the old favorite with a new nickname. Referred to by present day food critics as a "heart attack on a plate," it retains its popularity with reduced portions. If you would like to add a personal touch to Alfred D'Lelio's creation, try fresh sauteed mushrooms, which just happens to be a favorite of an Irish friend of mine.

3/4 pound fettuccine noodles, cooked al dente
1 stick unsalted butter
1 cup heavy cream
1 cup freshly grated Parmesan cheese
Freshly grated Parmesan cheese, for dusting
Coarsely ground fresh black pepper

While noodles are cooking, melt butter in saucepan large enough to accommodate the pasta with room to toss it without spilling. Over moderate heat, add noodles and mix very well with butter. Add half of the cream and toss with a fork and a spoon. Add half of the cheese to toss to incorporate well, adding more cream a little at a time but never too much. (The cream should hardly be noticeable when the dish is finished; use only enough to keep noodles from sticking together.) Keep tossing and add the rest of the cheese and, if needed, more cream. Toss until all the cheese is melted. Remove to heated serving plates and top with freshly grated cheese and a few turns of the pepper mill on coarse grade. Serve immediately.

Serves 4 to 6.

Note: A domestic Parmesan cheese is recommended, as it is not as sharp as imported Parmesan.

CORNISH PASTY

Lela Jacobson is known for making some of the best English-rooted Cornish pasties made in the state of Wisconsin. From her kitchen in Mineral Point, she prepares and serves them with her equally famous homemade chili sauce.

CRUST INGREDIENTS:

3 cups flour

1 teaspoon salt

1 cup (8 ounces) chilled lard, cut into small pieces

1 egg

Ice water

OTHER INGREDIENTS:

1 1/2 pounds cubed sirloin tip or round steak

4 cups thinly sliced potatoes

1 cup diced turnip or rutabaga (optional)

1/2 cup chopped onion

3 Tablespoons ground suet

1 Tablespoon salt

1 teaspoon black pepper

3 Tablespoons butter

Flour to make crust: Mix 3 cups flour and salt. Cut in lard until size of small peas. Break egg into measuring cup; mix lightly. Add enough ice water to measure 1 cup. Add egg mixture to flour, tossing lightly with a fork until dough forms. Wrap in plastic wrap or wax paper. Chill at least one hour. To make filling: Mix all remaining ingredients except butter and flour. To form and bake pasties: Preheat oven to 400 degrees. Grease one or two large baking pans. On a floured surface, divide dough into six equal portions. Roll out each portion into an 8- or 9-inch circle. Divide filling into six portions and place each portion on bottom half of each dough circle. Place 1/2 tablespoon of butter on each filling portion. Using extra flour to prevent sticking, fold dough over filling. Press to seal by folding small sections of dough to make a ropelike edge. Place on baking pans. Bake 15 minutes reduce heat to 375 degrees and bake additional 30-35 minutes. Serve with bottled or homemade chili sauce. Serves six big eaters.

LELA JACOBSON'S CHILI SAUCE

1 can (28 ounces) peeled tomatoes plus 1/2 cup V-8 vegetable juice, or 4 cups peeled, seeded fresh tomatoes
1/2 cup finely chopped onion
1/2 cup finely chopped celery
1/2 cup finely chopped sweet bell pepper (red or green)
1/2 cup apple cider vinegar
1/4 cup sugar
2 Tablespoons brown sugar
1 teaspoon salt
1/2 teaspoon whole celery seed
1/2 teaspoon whole mustard seed
1/2 teaspoon whole cloves
1-inch cinnamon stick

If using canned tomatoes, chop fine and combine with can juices and the vegetable juice in a heavy saucepan. If using fresh tomatoes, chop fine and measure into heavy saucepan. Add onion, celery and sweet pepper. Bring to hard simmer and cook, stirring often, until concentrated, about 30 minutes. Add vinegar, sugars, salt, celery seed and mustard seed. Tie cloves and cinnamon in cheesecloth or place in tea infuser. Add to sauce. Return to simmer. Reduce again until thick, about 1 hour. Remove spice bag. Serve hot or cold.

Yields 2 1/2 to 3 cups.

Note: Jacobson makes five quarts at a time, cans the cooked sauce in pints, processing them for 10 minutes in a boiling water bath.

KEITH STAHL'S 'CRUBCROCKERS'

Keith Stahl recalls "growing up" on krub in northern Michigan. Although he still makes them every month or so, his family refuses to eat the Scandinavian dumpling, often referring to them as "gut-pluggers". They also agree that one should wait at least two hours after consuming them before going for a swim.

1/3 pound lean salt pork, cut into small cubes
1/2 teaspoon allspice
1/4 teaspoon pepper
1/2 cup onions, cut fine
6 potatoes, finely ground
2 1/2 cups flour
1 Tablespoon cornstarch

Mix salt pork, onions, allspice and pepper in a separate bowl. In another bowl combine potatoes, flour and cornstarch. After mixing (mixture will be sticky) make into patties and fill with salt pork mixture. Form into a ball with mixture in the middle. Place in boiling water and cook uncovered for one hour. Serve with butter, salt and pepper.

Makes four.

OLDAY'S ANDERSON KRUB

The Olday household added a bit of Norwegian heritage
to the Sicilian, Italian, Jewish and Black neighborhood of
Milton Street in the old Greenbush neighborhood.
Suppers often included krub, an ethnic favorite the entire
family loved. Bill Olday and his brothers still get together
to make the dumplings and bring back a little bit of the
past and what they enjoyed as children.

5 pounds white potatoes
Flour
1 pound salt pork, cut in 1/4-inch cubes
3 to 4 gallons of water
Medium-size rutabaga, cut into 2-to-3-inch pieces
Butter

Grate potatoes, drain off juices and place in a large
bowl. Mix enough flour with potatoes until dumplings
can be formed into the size of a hard baseball. Heat water
in large kettle. Place rutabaga pieces in water with any
leftover salt pork cubes to give water a better flavor. Place
six 1/4-inch salt pork cubes in center of each dumpling
and place in cooking water. When dumplings begin to
float, usually in about 45 minutes or so, continue to cook
for an additional 20 minutes. Serve with butter chunks
on every bite, or with a milk gravy.

*Note: For leftovers, slice remaining dumplings and place in
greased fry pan to heat to your liking.*

Serve with butter chunks.

Southwestern Turnover (Empanadas)

One of many outstanding recipes featured in cookbooks written by local author Terese Allen, this was served for years at the Ovens of Brittany restaurant, much to the delight of customers.

3/4 pound boneless skinless chicken breasts
1/2 pound chorizo or hot Italian sausage
1 cup tomato salsa, or use bottled salsa
1 box (17 1/4 ounces) frozen, pre-rolled, ready-to-use puff pastry sheets (two sheets)
Flour
Egg white
2 cups grated Monterey jack cheese
Additional tomato salsa

To make filling: Cut chicken into very small pieces. Heat skillet, add chorizo and break it up with a fork as it cooks. When sausage is crumbly, add chicken and continue cooking until chicken is just tender. Drain well. Add salsa and chill thoroughly. If you plan to cook turnovers right after they are assembled, preheat oven to 350 degrees. Grease a cookie sheet. (Or you may assemble turnovers, refrigerate and bake later.) Carefully thaw puff pastry according to package instructions. Keep dough cold after it has thawed by returning it to the refrigerator until you are ready to assemble turnovers. On a floured surface, roll dough into two 14-inch x 9-inch sheets, and cut each into four 7-inch x 4 1/2-inch rectangles. Brush entire dough surface with egg white. Place 1/2 cup chicken/chorizo filling and 1/4 cup grated Monterey jack on bottom half of each rectangle. Fold top half over and press firmly along edges to seal the turnover. Trim the edges. Make one or two tiny slashes in the top of each turnover. Place on baking sheet. Bake 20-30 minutes until pastry is fully puffed and golden brown. Serve immediately, with additional salsa. Makes 8 turnovers.

Note: Chorizo is available at several food markets, including La Mexicana Market in Madison.

Chicken and Sour Cream Enchiladas

S.J. Martin, Madison, lost her favorite recipe which had taken first place for Conni Burgett in the Casserole category in the 1979 WSJ cookbook. Many readers responded with their clipping.

2 whole breasts of chicken

Two 10 3/4-ounce cans cream of onion soup

One 10 3/4-ounce can cream of chicken soup

One 4-ounce can chopped green chiles

3/4 cup onion, diced

1/4 teaspoon pepper

1/2 teaspoon salt

1 teaspoon white cooking wine (optional)

One 8-ounce carton sour cream

6 corn tortillas

1 pound Cheddar cheese

Boil chicken for 45 minutes to 1 hour, then set aside. Let cool. Combine all 3 cans of soup, green chilies, onion, salt, pepper and wine, and place over low heat. Remove skin and bones from chicken. Cut into bite-size pieces. Add to soup mixture. (Mixture should be like thick gravy. If too thick, milk may be added.) Add sour cream to mixture. (Original mixture may be heated as long as desired. However, sour cream should not be added until mixture is removed from heat.) Lightly grease 9-inch glass or metal baking dish with margarine or butter (do not use shortening). Layer bottom with 3 tortillas. Pour in half of the chicken mixture. Grate or slice cheese. Layer half of the cheese over chicken mixture. Repeat the procedure – tortillas, chicken mixture and cheese. Place in 350 degree oven and bake for 20-30 minutes.

Yield: 4 servings.

GEFILTE FISH

Submitted by Meyer Katz, LaCrosse, for Harva Hachten's "Flavor of Wisconsin" cookbook, this Jewish recipe is traditionally served with red (beet) horseradish.

3 pounds filleted fish: whitefish, trout, sheephead, carp (reserve bones, heads and tails)

6 large onions

2 large carrots

3 eggs, well-beaten

2 teaspoons matzo meal

Salt and pepper to taste

1/2 to 1 cup water

1 stalk celery, cut into pieces

Grind fish with three of the onions and one carrot, grated. Add eggs, matzo meal, salt and pepper and water. The finer the fish is ground, the fluffier the gefilte fish will be. Cook bones, heads and tails of fish, one onion, and salt to taste with water in a large kettle for one hour. Add remaining onions and carrot, both sliced, and celery. Bring to a boil. Make fish balls with hands moistened in cold water and lower gently into the boiling fish stock. Cover and simmer 1 1/2 to 2 hours, shaking the pot from time to time to keep the fish balls from sticking to the pan.

Dolmadakia
(Stuffed vine leaves)

I learned about Greek cooking from my neighbor, Kea Soldatos Peterson, whose parents emigrated from Greece many years ago to settle in Madison. Stuffed grapevine leaves, baklava, and spanakopita are just a sampling of the ethnic favorites served at the many family gatherings I attended as her guest.

One 16-ounce jar of grapevine leaves
1 onion, chopped
3/4 pound ground veal, round steak or lamb
2/3 cup uncooked rice
1/2 cup chicken broth or water
1 teaspoon crushed mint
2 teaspoons chopped parsley
1 teaspoon salt
Pepper to taste
2 Tablespoons olive oil
Chicken broth or water
Juice of 1 lemon

Carefully unfold the vine leaves and rinse under cold water. In bowl, combine onion, ground meat, uncooked rice, mint leaves, parsley, salt and pepper, olive oil and 1/2 cup chicken broth or water. Mix well. Form about 1 Tablespoon of mixture in an oval shape. Place on vine leaf and roll up. Repeat until all stuffing is used. Use a few leftover leaves and layer on bottom of pan. Place a layer of stuffed leaves very close together over the layer of leaves. Make another layer of leaves and continue layering until all stuffed leaves are tightly packed into pan. Pour enough broth or water to barely cover vine leaves, then add lemon juice. Weigh down stuffed leaves with a flat plate. Cover pan and bring to boil over moderate heat and simmer slowly for 1 hour. Serve cold or hot with Avgolemono Sauce. These are excellent as an appetizer or an accompaniment to an entree.

Serves four or more.

Avgolemono Saltsa
(Egg Lemon Sauce)

3 eggs, separated
Juice of 2 lemons
1 cup broth or stock
1 Tablespoon cornstarch

Beat egg whites until stiff; add egg yolks and continue beating; add lemon juice very slowly, beating constantly so the sauce does not curdle. Thicken hot chicken broth with cornstarch dissolved in a little water, slowly add boiling stock to egg mixture, beating constantly until smooth and creamy.

Makes 2 cups.

Note: This is a basic sauce in Greek cooking either poured over vegetables, fish or meats. Recipe is from "Greek Cooking for the Gods" by Eva Zane.

BLACK BEANS AND RICE

The very heart and soul of evening meals in Key West, black beans and rice made an ethnic statement when I lived in Florida in the late 1950s. It was a sleepy little island town complemented with Cuban flavors, Cuban music, louvered hurricane shutters and tropical foliage. I can only hope that much of it remains as it was. Black beans are slowly simmered to a soft, thick stew, and the Piquant Sauce, or Sofrito, is added during the final minutes of cooking.

1 pound black beans, washed and picked over
1 bay leaf
Salt and pepper
2 cloves garlic, peeled and finely chopped
1 onion, peeled and finely chopped
1/2 teaspoon crumbled oregano
6 cups steamed white rice

Soak the beans overnight in enough water to cover. Add the bay leaf and bring to a boil in the soaking water, skimming the surface if necessary. Add a bit of salt and freshly ground pepper plus the garlic, onion and oregano. Simmer, covered, for about 2 to 3 hours (cooking time varies a great deal depending on the beans) or until the beans are rather mushy. Watch the kettle continually toward the end, stirring and adding a bit of water to keep the beans from scorching or sticking. During the last hour of cooking time, remove the bay leaf and add Piquant Sauce (see recipe below). Have 6 cups of hot, cooked white rice ready to serve. Ladle beans over rice and serve hot.

Makes 8 to 10 servings.

(Recipe from "The Best of Ethnic Home Cooking," by Mary Poulos Wilde.)

Piquant Sauce

- 1/2 cup olive oil
  1 clove garlic, minced
  1 onion, finely chopped
  1 large green bell pepper, finely chopped
  4-ounce jar of fire-roasted pimientos, chopped
  1/2 teaspoon crumbled oregano
  Pinch dried thyme
  2 to 3 tablespoons cider vinegar, or to taste. Combine all ingredients in saucepan and simmer very slowly, stirring often, until vegetables are really soft, but not brown. Stir this mixture into the beans during the last 15 minutes of cooking time.

Amish Vanilla Pie

A pie to remember a special group of people who dedicate their lives to the land where they live.

FILLING:

1/2 cup brown sugar

1 Tablespoon flour, rounded

1/4 cup dark corn syrup

1 1/2 teaspoons vanilla

1 egg, beaten

1 cup water

TOPPING:

1 cup flour

1/2 cup brown sugar

1/2 teaspoon cream of tartar

1/2 teaspoon baking soda

1/4 cup butter

One 9-inch unbaked pie shell

Mix the filling ingredients and cook until boiling and thickened. Cool. Combine topping until crumbly. Pour cooled pudding into pie shell and top with crumb mixture. Bake at 350 degrees for 40 minutes or until golden brown.

SCHMARREN

Because spellings and names change with dialect, Ria Suchomel, Sun Prairie, told me that in Austria this would be known as Kaiser Schmarren.

2 hard rolls

Milk

2 1/2 ounces butter

1 1/2 ounces sugar

2 eggs, separated

A little lemon rind

Use rolls at least two days old; soak in milk until soft, squeezing out all moisture. Cream butter, sugar and lemon rind. Add egg yolks, then rolls. Fold in beaten egg whites and place mixture in a buttered casserole to bake at 350 degrees until brown.

Note: One tablespoon of raisins and some chopped walnuts can also be added. Suchomel often adds the eggs whole and, instead of baking it in the oven, fries the mixture in a buttered heavy frying pan as you would hash brown potatoes.

BLOTKAKE
WHIPPED CREAM CAKE

When a reader asked for a strawberry dessert to serve to guests at a Norwegian dinner party, I contacted Jerry Paulson for help. As a member of the Sons of Norway and one who has taught Norwegian cooking classes, Paulson thought this would be perfect for company since it can be made ahead and refrigerated.

6 large eggs
3/4 cup sugar
1 cup flour
Milk (see note)
FILLING:
4 cups whipped cream
1/2 teaspoon vanilla
1 Tablespoon powdered sugar
1 to 2 cups strawberries, cut

Beat eggs and sugar for 10 minutes, until stiff at high speed. Gently add sifted flour. Pour into greased and floured 10-inch springform pan. Bake in center of oven at 325 degrees for 30 minutes. Do not remove for 5 minutes, leaving oven door open. Remove from pan when completely cool. Cut cake into 2 or 3 layers. Sprinkle each layer with some of the milk. Whip cream and add powdered sugar and vanilla. Mix berries with 2/3 of the whipped cream and spread between layers. Use remaining whipped cream for frosting. Reserve some of berries whole for decorating cake after frosted. Refrigerate until served.

Note: One Tablespoon or more of milk is used to sprinkle over cake to prevent from drying before whipped cream is used.

Vareniki

With fond recollections, Anita Pierce, Boulder Junction, wondered if I could find a recipe for fruit dumplings like her grandmother used to make many years ago. This recipe, described as Russian dessert dumplings, was found in the Minnesota Heritage cookbook.

4 to 5 cups sifted flour, depending on size of eggs
3 eggs
1 teaspoon salt
1/2 cup water
1 quart water for boiling
1 teaspoon salt
1/4 cup melted butter
Sour cream, optional
Sugar, optional
FILLING:
3 cups pitted cherries, chopped
1/2 cup sugar
2 Tablespoons flour

Put flour into large mixing bowl. Make a deep hollow in the flour and put eggs, 1 teaspoon salt and 1/2 cup water in center. Slowly combine and knead to make a stiff dough. If too crumbly, add a bit more water. Let dough stand for 45 minutes. Form two logs about 2 inches in diameter. Slice logs into 1/2-inch circles and roll out into 1/2-inch thick rounds. Mix filling ingredients together and place a spoonful on one half of each circle and fold over to form a half circle. Pinch edges together to seal. Drop Vareniki into boiling, salted water and simmer, uncovered, for 8-10 minutes or until they rise to the surface. Remove, drain and place on shallow platter. Pour melted butter on top and serve hot. Top with sour cream and sugar, if desired.

Yield: about 3 dozen.

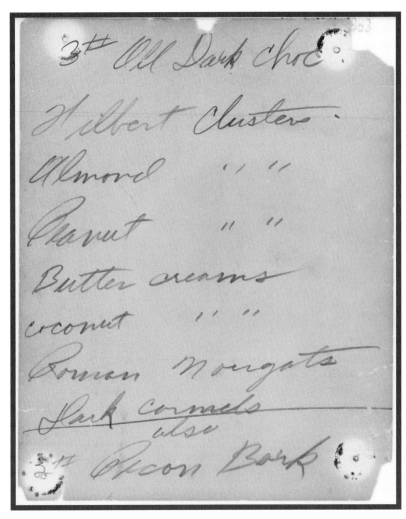

Old paper found in the basement of the Chocolate Shop.

Sweet chocolate dreams

. . . . ●

CHANTAL COADY'S CONNECTION TO CHOCOLATE BEGAN AT A YOUNG AGE WHEN HER MOTHER USED CADBURY MILK TRAY BARS AS A BRIBE TO ATTEND SATURDAY CATECHISM CLASSES WITH A SISTER AND BROTHER. The most difficult decision of all occurred after each class was dismissed and it was time to make a selection from the many shapes of chocolate candies and the variety of colors and flavors each held inside. Fondness for the product of the cocoa bean continued to blossom with age, and today Coady is not only co-founder of the Chocolate Society and author of "Chocolate, Food of the Gods," but also proprietor of Rococo, one of London's finest chocolate shops. I suspect she would have been as fascinated with "our" Chocolate Shop in Madison, just as we all were.

Chocolate was the prized ingredient for sweet pleasures concocted in a minuscule Willie Wonka world at 548 State St., where Fritz Ragatz's Oriental Specialties Shop is today. Just open the heavy door, walk across the small black and white square tiles and, suddenly, you were surrounded by pyramids of freshly made, hand-dipped chocolates protected behind showcases of polished wood and glass. When I was young I gravitated toward the chocolate-covered cherries, my favorite to this day. However, I remember wishing that someday, when I grew up, I would have enough money to order one of everything. An innocent dream of a sweet-toothed youngster. At the rear of the store, on the mezzanine, were booths of the same well-tended varnished wood, where sundaes, sodas and malts were served on heavy white mottled marble. It was there where I first experienced a Hot Milk Swiss Miss Sundae in a tulip glass, never seeing it offered anywhere else since then. The Chocolate Shop was built in 1909, not for ice cream sundaes and chocolate candies, but for Mead and Hunt Architect and Engineers. The character of the building changed when the Chocolate Shop moved in, but there remains, after all these years, a remnant of the past on the front, a facade of gneiss (pronounced "nice"), the oldest known material to exist on Earth. UW-Madison geology students are encouraged by their professors to stop by to inspect the granitelike rock that resembles marble. When Ragatz brought imported Oriental flavor to replace the tasty treats dreams are made of, he discovered a box in the basement filled with Syracuse china, decorated with an orange and black floral pattern, once used for customers. Attached to a basement wall was a handwritten reminder for nuts, coconut, almond bark, butter creams and Roman nougats, with the name and address of a South LaSalle Street location in Chicago. The heavy, stone candy-making table also remains with other candy and ice cream-making equipment, but the kitchen has become Ragatz's office with files and folders replacing copper pots and long-handled stirrers. Several calls and letters have arrived from readers who remember, as many do, the State Street of yesterday and the mouth-watering creations served at 548 State St., such as the Chocolate Shop Chocolate Torte and their never-to-be-forgotten hot fudge sauce.

ORIGINAL CHOCOLATE HOUSE FUDGE SAUCE

Shortly following a request for the Chocolate Shop's fudge sauce, a letter arrived with the recipe stating that it had been passed on through the years by a friend who had worked there and had "taken an oath" never to reveal the shop's secrets. Revealing this one will please the half of Madisonians who left a part of their heart there after a single visit.

2 squares of melted unsweetened chocolate

2 Tablespoons butter

3/4 cup white sugar

One 5-ounce can of evaporated milk

Melt chocolate and butter together. Add sugar and stir. Add milk gradually and cook until it comes to a gentle boil. Simmer for a minute or so or until thick and creamy.

Note: Although stirring is not mentioned in the directions, I would suggest doing so to make certain it combines well and does not burn or stick to the bottom of the pan.

BEACON HILL BROWNIES

Jerry Paulson offered to trade a good Norwegian recipe for a rich, heavy, moist, chocolate brownie recipe. I knew immediately which one I would share with him. Paulson and his friends then had a "brownie" contest. Just as I promised, this one won hands down.

8 ounces unsweetened chocolate
1 cup butter, room temperature
5 eggs
3 cups sugar
1 Tablespoon vanilla
1 1/2 cups flour
1 1/2 to 2 cups coarsely broken walnuts

Melt together chocolate and butter over low heat. Stir to combine, and cool. Beat eggs, sugar and vanilla for 10 minutes in electric mixer. Blend in cooled chocolate mixture. Add flour and stir in by hand just until blended. Fold in broken walnuts. Place in greased 9x13-inch pan and bake at 375 degrees for 35 to 40 minutes. Be careful not to overbake as brownies will dry. Top should be dull and "cracked" around edges. Cool on wire rack. Frost with dark chocolate frosting, if desired. Cut when cool. Delicious with ice cream.

Yield: 24 2-inch brownies.

Note: When I made these I noticed that the brownies did not have cracked edges. In fact, the top was almost perfect except for a crack in one place. Ovens may vary, so bake accordingly.

CHOCOLATE DECADENCE

After a few requests for chocolate decadence cake, I opened Natalie Haughton's 365 Great Recipes for Chocolate Desserts and found this heavenly concoction that should please all chocolate lovers.

1 pound semisweet or bittersweet chocolate, cut up

1 stick (4 ounces) butter

4 eggs

1 Tablespoon flour

Whipped cream and fresh raspberries, optional

Preheat oven to 425 degrees. In a 1-quart glass bowl, combine chocolate, butter and 1 Tablespoon hot water. Heat in microwave oven on high two minutes, or until chocolate is melted and smooth when stirred. Set aside. In a large bowl, beat eggs three to four minutes with an electric mixer on high speed until thickened and increased in volume. Beat in flour and chocolate mixture until well blended. Spread evenly in an 8-inch springform pan buttered and lined with parchment or wax paper. Bake 12 to 15 minutes. Cake will be soft in center, but will firm up when cold. Let stand until cool, then refrigerate until serving time. Run sharp knife around edge of cake and remove springform side.

Serve slices topped with whipped cream and fresh raspberries, when available.

Makes eight to 10 servings.

CHOCOLATE DROPS

Vicki Pearcy was craving an old-fashioned chocolate drop cookie like those her mother used to make. This recipe was a Blue Ribbon winner from the McLean County Fair held in North Dakota and later featured in a 1968 cookbook, Favorite Recipes of America.

1/2 cup soft shortening, part butter
1 cup sugar
1 egg
2 ounces melted chocolate
3/4 cup buttermilk or sour milk
1 teaspoon vanilla
1 3/4 cups flour
1/2 teaspoon baking soda
1/2 teaspoon salt
1 cup chopped pecans or other nuts.

Preheat oven to 400 degrees. Mix shortening, sugar, egg and chocolate thoroughly; stir in buttermilk and vanilla. Blend flour, soda and salt; add. Mix in nuts, chill for at least 1 hour. Drop by rounded teaspoonfuls 2 inches apart onto lightly greased baking sheet. Bake 8 to 10 minutes or until cookie springs back when lightly touched. Cool.

Yield: 3 1/2 dozen.

FROSTING:

1 Tablespoon butter
1 square unsweetened chocolate
1 1/2 Tablespoon warm water
1 cup sifted confectioners' sugar

Blend butter, chocolate and warm water in bowl, place over hot water; beat in confectioners' sugar. Spread over cookies.

FUDGE MELTAWAYS

Longtime Madisonians still miss being able to call Madison Gas & Electric home economists for questions that needed answers and for advice when cooking or baking a particular recipe. All that is left today are the wonderful holiday cooking handbooks that found loyal homes on our kitchen shelves. Patrick Regan remembers the fudge meltaways featured in the 1960 compilation, and so do an endless list of readers. This is so simple, and so good.

Heat oven to 350 degrees. Prepare batter for cakelike brownies directed on fudge brownie mix package (1 pound, 6 ounces) except bake in greased jellyroll pan, 15x10-inch, 20 to 25 minutes. Cool. Frost with vanilla ready-to-spread frosting. When frosting is firm, spread with 3 envelopes (1 ounce each) premelted chocolate. Chill. Before chocolate is completely firm, cut into 1 1/2-inch squares.

Hot Fudge
Sundae Sauce

Almost every good cook is aware of the quality of recipes found in Farm Journal publications. Cherished for years as "cooking bibles," the books cover a wide range of food items and preparation. One book featuring favorites from County Fairs ended my own longtime search for the ultimate in hot fudge sauce. I have used this recipe for at least 20 years and renew my love for it over and over again as a perfect dinner party dessert by drizzling it over coffee ice cream before a garnish of freshly butter-roasted, salted pecan halves.

One 14 1/2-ounce can of evaporated milk

2 cups sugar

4 squares unsweetened chocolate

1/4 cup butter or regular margarine

1 1/2 teaspoons vanilla

1/4 teaspoon salt

Combine milk and sugar in a saucepan. Bring to a full rolling boil, stirring occasionally. Boil, stirring, 1 minute. Add chocolate. Stir until melted. Beat over heat until smooth. Remove from heat and stir in butter, vanilla and salt. Serve hot or cold. Store in refrigerator.

Makes about 3 cups.

FOR THE LOVE OF CHOCOLATE

Not one to give up on a request, I kept searching for a dense chocolate cake totally void of flour. This appeared in an issue of the Ladies Home Journal magazine, shared by Chef Knut Apitz of Grenadier's Restaurant in Milwaukee.

6 large eggs, separated
1 1/4 pounds semisweet chocolate
12 Tablespoons unsalted butter
2 Tablespoons sugar
1 Tablespoon coffee-flavored liqueur
Pinch of salt
Whipped cream
Chocolate or custard sauce, optional
Fresh raspberries; optional

Preheat oven to 400 degrees. Separate eggs, placing whites in large mixing bowl. Melt chocolate, butter and sugar in a double boiler until smooth. Remove from heat; whisk in egg yolks one at a time and add coffee-flavored liqueur. Beat egg whites with a pinch of salt to soft peaks. Gently fold whites into chocolate mixture. Pour into 9-inch springform pan. Bake 18 to 20 minutes, until center is just set. Cool on a wire rack. (Can be made ahead and refrigerated for up to two days. Serve at room temperature.) Serve with a dollop of whipped cream to show off the deep chocolate flavor of this rich, dense cake. For a more elaborate dessert, serve with chocolate sauce and garnish with fresh raspberries.

CHOCOLATE MELT-AWAYS

Yet another chocolate cookie from the Madison Gas & Electric Company. A tried and true favorite of yesterday. . . and today.

1 cup butter
1 1/4 cups powdered sugar
1 teaspoon vanilla
1 1/4 cups all-purpose flour
1/2 teaspoon salt; 1 cup walnuts, grated
9 ounces sweet milk chocolate, melted

Cream butter. Gradually add powdered sugar. Cream well; add vanilla. Sift flour and salt together. Add sifted dry ingredients and grated walnuts. Melt chocolate over hot water. Blend into above mixture.

Chill. Shape into balls, using 1 teaspoon of dough. Place on greased cookie sheet, allowing space for cookies to spread while baking. Bake at 250 degrees about 40 minutes.

Makes about 11 dozen cookies.

Bourbon Balls

Years ago, Madison Gas & Electric compiled favorite recipes of staff members to fill small handy cookbooks published just in time for the holiday seasons. Bourbon balls was featured in their 1956 collection and it has been a favorite ever since.

1 cup vanilla wafer crumbs
1 cup finely chopped pecans
1 cup sifted powdered sugar
2 Tablespoons cocoa
1/4 cup bourbon
1 1/2 Tablespoons light corn syrup
Powdered sugar for coating

Combine dry ingredients. Blend bourbon and corn syrup. Mix all ingredients and shape into 1-inch balls. Roll in sifted powdered sugar. Refrigerate.

Makes about 4 dozen.

Note: Bourbon, brandy or rum can be used. The confection can also be rolled in finely chopped nuts, if desired. Store in tightly covered container at least three days. They improve with age.

Slices Of Sin

When the cook of a local well-known eating establishment headed northeast for Door County, a repertoire of great recipes went with her, one being a favorite of Mary Knoll. Shortly thereafter, another reader contacted me with a description of a flourless chocolate cake her family enjoyed at a ski lodge in Colorado.

Attempting to please both, I settled for this one featured in a publication of America's best recipes from community cookbooks.

Eight 1-ounce squares semisweet chocolate
1/2 cup strong brewed coffee
1 cup butter
1 cup sugar
4 eggs
1 cup whipped cream
2 to 3 teaspoons brandy

Line an 8 1/2x4 1/2-inch glass loaf pan with aluminum foil; grease foil with butter. Set aside. Combine chocolate and coffee in top of a double boiler. Bring water to a boil; reduce heat to low, and cook until chocolate melts, stirring occasionally. Add butter and sugar to melted chocolate mixture, stirring until butter melts. Let cool. Add eggs, one at a time, beating well after each addition. Pour batter into prepared loaf pan. Bake at 350 degrees for 35 to 45 minutes or until a crust forms on top. Let cool completely on a wire rack. Cover tightly; chill at least 2 days. When ready to serve: Beat whipped cream until soft peaks form. Gently fold in brandy. Unmold cake onto a serving platter.

Serve with whipped cream.

Yield: 10 to 12 servings.

Mike Tripalin with his daughters, Catherine and
Elaine at Vilas Park, summer – 1940.

Father's Day
desserts

. . . . •

A FEW YEARS AGO MY FATHER TOLD ME THAT WHEN ONE REACHES HIS AGE, ALL THAT REMAINS ARE THE MEMORIES. When you're 90, that means a lifetime. This Sunday my family will celebrate, with Daddy, another Father's Day with memories that began for us in the '30s and '40s. We took the good times for granted because every day together was filled with excitement.

Daddy's heart was as big as the hand that led us – "his little girls"– from Vilas Park on warm Sunday afternoons to ankle-deep wading along the shoreline at Tenney Park. We held tightly as he guided us on hikes through the upper and lower "Indian" trails that wove two paths through trees and bushes on the periphery of Lakeland Avenue, and we knew his hands were within reach when we rode Lake Mendota waves on black inner tubes down at Sandy Beach, today known as Warner Park beach. During autumn, when the parks were ablaze with color, together we explored the treasures that awaited on cliffs at Hoyt Park at the end of Regent Street. When winter arrived, Sundays were spent sledding or tobogganing down the snow-packed hills of Olbrich Park and Blackhawk Country Club. At the bottom of each hill he'd grab the rope to pull us back up to the top, only to repeat the thrill over and over until we were cold and ready to go home. Being the ice skater he was, we were held high in his arms as he enjoyed the splendor of winter on the Tenney Park lagoons. When the Italians of Greenbush held picnics at Brittingham Park, we were led through the area where he had played as a child, to be introduced to the old friends and the families he knew well. Along the way, he treated us to a taste of our heritage with fennel-studded homemade sausages grilled to a toasty brown, and cannoli "just like Grandma used to make." Each

- Sunday was a celebration of togetherness; each Sunday became a day to remember. Receiving gifts on Father's Day was never important to Daddy. He wanted nothing more than to be together. To him, family was the greatest gift of all. Yet, as little girls, we saved coins for shopping trips to the Ben Franklin store on Atwood Avenue, our first purchase being a circle of soap for his shaving mug and brush. Later, we switched to socks. Ties, shirts and summer pajamas were purchased a few blocks away, from Ole Olson at Ole's Clothes Shop, and even later, shiny new golf balls and fishing lures from Wes Lefebvre at Berg-Peterson Sporting Goods across the street from the dime store. A hybrid rosebush, red geraniums, garden gloves. Flagstad's knew well of Daddy's summer hobbies. And now, at 90, what does he need? The mug and brush have been replaced with an electric shaver. The golf bag rests in the basement. Someone else owns the boat, and the flowers we buy are planted with our garden gloves. Although he claims that all he wants is continued good health and to be with family, we know of something that would bring another twinkle to his eye. Pie. Flaky crust, smooth creamy filling, sliced bananas tucked inside. Except for cannoli, banana cream and coconut cream pies have always been his favorite dessert. As simple as it sounds, to bake one, then share a slice with him on Father's Day is really what good memories and life is all about.

Sour Cream Blueberry Pie– Norske Nook, Osseo

Osseo needs no introduction to hometown cooking enthusiasts and pie connoisseurs who have stopped by for a minute or a meal. Owner Jerry Bechard has created a niche to keep everyone happy with an endless supply of 10-inch homemade pies covered with flaky crust, whipped cream, or meringue piled higher than you've ever seen before. The restaurant, a favorite of Wisconsin travelers, is the kind of place you wish were right around the corner within walking distance from home.

1 baked single 10-inch pie crust
2 cups sour cream
4 egg yolks
1 3/4 cups sugar
4 heaping teaspoons flour
1 1/2 cups chopped peeled apples, preferably McIntosh
2 cups wild Maine blueberries (see note)
2 cups whipping cream, whipped
Confectioners' sugar
Vanilla to taste

Stir sour cream in egg yolks in heavy saucepan. Add sugar, flour and chopped apples and mix. Cook over medium heat until filling is glossy and thick, or about 5 minutes after a full boil. Remove from heat. Clean blueberries and add to mixture. Let cool. Place in cooled crust and allow to cool completely. Top with whipped cream sweetened with confectioners' sugar and vanilla, to taste.

Note: If using a can of blueberries, drain, leaving some juice to create a purple-blue color.

Fruit Cheese Pie—
Burnstad's, Tomah

Often referred to as the "best known secret in Wisconsin," Burnstad's rely on bottom-of-the-heart family and employee dedication that brings people from hundreds of miles away to visit their unique European Village establishment, extraordinary grocery store, and the food they are proud of serving in their restaurants. Pies made on the premises are more than tantalizing. One look and you know that whatever you order you must leave room for dessert. One taste, and you know you'll be back for more.

One (10-inch) baked pie crust

FILLING:

One (8-ounce) package cream cheese

One (14-ounce) can sweetened condensed milk

1 teaspoon vanilla

1/3 cup fresh lemon juice.

Mix until blended well. Pour in baked pie crust. Chill 4 hours.

1 pint fresh strawberries

1/2 cup strawberry glaze (can be purchased)

1 pint fresh blueberries

1/4 cup corn syrup

Whipped cream, optional

Wash strawberries and pat dry. Hull and quarter. Fold glaze into berries and pile in the center of pie. Wash and pat dry the blueberries; coat with corn syrup. Pour around the outer edge of pie crust, surrounding strawberries. Serve with dollop of whipped cream.

Note: Peeled and sliced kiwi, also coated with corn syrup, can be used to decorate pie. If using peaches or other fruit in season to surround berries, coat with corn syrup to glaze as blueberries were.

CLIFF HOUSE
CHOCOLATE PECAN PIE

This is a perfect way to end a celebration any time of the year, especially if one is craving chocolate. and pecans. Named for the Cliff House in San Francisco, the recipe was discovered in Ghiradelli's Original Chocolate Cookbook when a reader was in search of something similar.

1 (4-ounce) bar Ghirardelli Bittersweet Chocolate
1/4 cup butter or margarine
2/3 cup light corn syrup
3 eggs
1 Tablespoon vanilla or bourbon
1/4 teaspoon salt
1/2 cup packed brown sugar
1 cup pecans, chopped or left as halves
9-inch unbaked pie shell

In heavy saucepan, melt broken chocolate with butter and corn syrup, stirring constantly until smooth (or microwave 2-3 miuntes on medium, stirring twice.) Beat eggs slightly with vanilla and salt; stir in chocolate mixture and nuts. Pour into pie shell. Bake at 400 degrees for 10 minutes. Reduce heat to 350 degrees and continue to bake 30 to 35 minutes; cool. Serve with whipped cream, if desired.

Makes 6 to 8 servings.

Coconut Banana Cream Pie

If I asked my father what kind of pie he'd like to have for a Father's Day dessert, he'd say either Coconut Cream or Banana. A 1994 issue of Country Woman magazine, a simply delightful publication from Greendale, Wis. solved the "problem" of which one to bake by featuring the best of both with this prize winning recipe.

CRUST:

3 cups flaked coconut

7 Tablespoons butter or margarine

2 large firm bananas, sliced

Whipped cream and sliced bananas, optional

FILLING:

3/4 cup sugar

1/4 cup all-purpose flour

3 Tablespoons cornstarch

1/4 teaspoon salt

3 cups light cream

4 egg yolks, lightly beaten

2 teaspoons vanilla extract

In a skillet, saute coconut in butter until golden. Press all but 2 Tablespoons into the bottom and up sides of a greased 9-inch pie plate. Bake at 350 degrees for 7 minutes. In a saucepan, combine the sugar, flour, cornstarch and salt. Gradually add cream and bring to a boil. Cook and stir constantly for 2 minutes. Add a small amount to egg yolks. Return all to pan; cook for 2 minutes. Remove from heat; add vanilla. Cool to room temperature. Place bananas in crust. Cover with cream mixture. Chill until set, about 2 hours. Sprinkle with reserved coconut. If desired, garnish with whipped cream and bananas.

Coconut Cream Pie—
Main Street Cafe, Siren

As cozy place that fits hundreds of small town cafe molds serving endless cups of coffee to sip on while discussing local and national news is the Main Street Cafe in Siren. Owner Connie Daeffler's pies are prepared before the door is unlocked in the morning and, if you are lucky, you'll savor a piece by nightfall before it disappears.

9-inch baked pie shell
3 cups of 2% milk
1/4 teaspoon salt
3/4 cup sugar
1/3 cup cornstarch
1/2 teaspoon vanilla
2 Tablespoons butter
3 egg yolks
A "handful" of coconut, about 1/2 cup

Heat milk. In bowl, mix dry ingredients. Pour in 1/2 cup warm milk and egg yolks. Add to remaining warm milk and stir until thick. Add butter and vanilla. Fold in coconut. Pour into baked pie shell and allow to cool before piling meringue over filling.

MERINGUE:
10 egg whites at room temperature
1/4 teaspoon cream of tartar
1 cup powdered sugar

Beat eggs until almost stiff. Add cream of tartar and powdered sugar and beat until stiff. Top with extra coconut and bake at 325 degrees for about 10 minutes or until golden brown.

Sour Cream Raisin Pie, Robertson's Family Restaurant, Spooner

The phrase, "I'd sooner go to Spooner" must have been uttered with Robertson's restaurant in mind. I heard once that Sundays at Robertson's are so busy that it is nothing to empty 26 pie tins before nightfall. The restaurant is a family operation that exudes friendliness and sparkles throughout the day from breakfast through evening dinners. With a view from the back windows of the spectacular new state fish hatchery, one can sit just a little bit longer to relax with a piece of pie and an extra cup of coffee.

1 3/4 cups raisins
1 cup half and half
3 egg yolks, reserving whites for meringue
Pinch of salt
4 Tablespoons flour
1/2 cup brown sugar
1/4 teaspoon nutmeg
1/2 teaspoon cinnamon
1/2 teaspoon vanilla
2 Tablespoons butter
2 heaping Tablespoons sour cream
One (9-inch) baked pie shell

Put raisins in saucepan, cover with water. Cook until water evaporates. Set aside. Combine half and half, egg yolks, salt, flour, brown sugar, nutmeg and cinnamon. Whip with wire whisk until smooth. Add to raisins and cook until thick. Remove from heat; add vanilla and sour cream. Cool slightly in pan. Pour into pie shell and top with meringue made with leftover egg whites.

Raspberry Cream Cheese Pie—
Main Street Cafe, Bloomer

Owner Don Stoik likes to remind his customers to leave the room for what he considers to be the very best way to end a meal. The tower of pies greeting each customer who enters the cafe is a reminder of his dessert litany. During raspberry season the early morning Main Street Cafe bakers go through 300 pounds of berries to keep their customers happy with a recipe that placed first in a recent statewide restaurant pie contest. During Thanksgiving, busy homemakers rely on Stoik's pies to please their families. . . after turkey, mashed potatoes and gravy has been served.

Cream cheese filling

4 ounces cream cheese

4 ounces powdered sugar

4 ounces whipped cream topping

Cream together cheese and powdered sugar. Mix in whipped cream topping and spread in bottom of baked 10-inch pie shell.

GLAZE:

1 cup water

2/3 cup sugar

1/3 cup cornstarch

1/3 cup raspberry Jell-O

1 1/2 to 2 cups fresh raspberries

Heat water, sugar and cornstarch and stir until mixture thickens. Remove from heat and add raspberry Jell-O. Fold in raspberries. Carefully place on cheese base. Chill and serve.

STRAWBERRY PIE

A favorite from the strawberry fields of Wisconsin and the recipe card file of Bernice Sewell, Richland Center.

CRUST:

1 cup flour

1 stick margarine

2 Tablespoons sugar

Mix with fork and press into pie pan. Bake for 15 minutes at 350 degrees and cool before filling.

FILLING:

1 cup water 1 cup sugar

2 Tablespoons cornstarch

2 Tablespoons strawberry Jell-O

Fresh strawberries, left whole, stems removed

Whipped cream

Cook water, sugar and cornstarch in saucepan until clear. Add strawberry Jell-O while still hot. Cool. Fill cooled baked pie shell with fresh strawberries. Pour cooled mixture over berries; refrigerate. Serve with whipped cream.

Elderberry-Apple Pie

Ruth Jungbluth's mother, Eunice M. Yeager, passed along this recipe to her family at least 50 years ago. Since then it has been a favorite at church auctions and bake sales. However, the number of pies baked depends on picking the elderberries before the birds have their annual feast.

Pastry for a two crust 9 or 10- inch pie
2 1/2 to 3 1/2 cups apples, peeled, cored and sliced (according to pie size)
1 cup ripe elderberries, washed and stemmed
1 Tablespoon fresh lemon juice
1 to 1 1/2 cups sugar
2 Tablespoons flour
Dash of salt

Line pie pan with pastry crust. In large bowl, mix sliced apples and elderberries. Sprinkle with lemon juice. In another bowl, mix sugar (vary amount according to size of pie, tartness of apples, and individual taste) flour and salt. Add to apple mixture, put in crust and cover with top crust. Cut 2 or 3 slits in top crust. Bake for 15 minutes at 425 degrees; reduce heat to 375 degrees and bake additional 30 to 40 minutes until bubbly.

Note: If elderberries are unavailable, blueberries can be substituted.

MOM'S GRAHAM CRACKER PIE

I used to order this pie every time I had lunch at the Hoffman House on East Washington Avenue. It was billowy, delicious and so easy to remember. Their recipe has disappeared with time, but a similar one was found in the "New Glarus Swiss United Church of Christ Cookbook," submitted, with pride, by Mary Jane Wagner.

16 squares graham crackers
1 teaspoon flour
1/3 cup sugar
1 teaspoon cinnamon
1/3 cup melted butter
1/2 cup sugar
2 Tablespoons cornstarch
3 egg yolks
2 cups milk
3/4 teaspoon vanilla
3 egg whites
6 Tablespoons sugar
1/4 teaspoon cream of tartar

Crush graham crackers very fine and mix with next 4 ingredients. Reserve 1/3 cup of crumb mixture. Rest of mixture is patted into 9-inch pie pan. Whip egg yolks in a large 6- to 8-cup bowl. Mix in 1/2 cup sugar, cornstarch, milk and vanilla. Cook in microwave 6 to 8 minutes, stirring every 2 minutes or until pudding coats spoon. Pour in pie shell. Beat egg whites, 6 tablespoons sugar and cream of tartar until stiff peaks form. Cover pie with meringue and sprinkle with 1/3 cup mix of crumbs. Bake at 400 degree until brown, about 8-10 minutes.

Green Tomato Mincemeat

Our summers are never long enough to ripen all the fruit from the vines. Be thrifty and use what is leftover in your garden for this homey flavor of rural America. This particular recipe, clipped in the mid-1970s from the Wisconsin State Journal, had been a favorite of California resident Larry Sperling. Dale Bruhn Madison, responded with the exact recipe—the same one he uses each year to make tassies, tarts and bars.

3 pounds green tomatoes, thinly sliced (about 2 quarts sliced)
1/4 cup salt
2 large apples, cored and chopped but unpeeled
1 large orange, seeded and chopped but unpeeled
1 15-ounce package seedless raisins, about 2 1/2 cups
1 cup sugar
1 pint dark corn syrup
2 Tablespoons pumpkin pie spice

Sprinkle tomatoes with salt as you layer them in a bowl; cover and let stand at room temperature overnight. Rinse with cold water and drain well. Chop fine. Into a 4-quart saucepot turn the tomatoes, apple, orange, raisins, sugar, corn syrup and spice. Cover and simmer 45 minutes. Uncover and boil gently, stirring occasionally, for 1 hour 15 minutes. Store in appropriate containers in the freezer. Makes 2 1/2 pints – enough for two 9-inch pies. To make pies: Stir 1/4 cup light or golden rum into 2 1/2 cups Green Tomato Mincemeat; cover and let stand at room temperature overnight. Turn into an unbaked 9-inch pastry shell; cover with vented top crust. Bake in a preheated 425 degree oven 45 to 50 minutes.

Lemon Meringue Pie– Island City Cafe, Cumberland

Heavily populated with Italians, it is expected that the island city of Cumberland has restaurants that serve spaghetti, stores that offer homemade Italian sausage, and liquor stores with an ample supply of red wine to serve wtih either. I happen to know that Italians also have a fondness for lemon meringue pie. Many thanks to owner Debbie Svik for sharing the tart lemon favorite that pleases both local residents and those traveling through town who need to stop for lunch or dinner.

3 cups sugar
6 Tablespoons flour
6 Tablespoons cornstarch
Dash of salt
1 1/2 cups water
6 eggs, separated
4 Tablespoons butter
4 teaspoons shredded lemon peel
2/3 cup lemon juice, fresh or bottled

Combine sugar, flour, cornstarch and dash of salt in saucepan. Stir in 1 1/2 cups water and cook over medium high heat until bubbly and thick. Reduce heat, cooking 2 to 3 minutes more. Remove from heat. Beat egg yolks. Stir 1 cup hot filling into egg yolks, then return this mixture to saucepan and bring entire mixture back to boil; cook 2 additional minutes, boiling gently. Remove from heat. Stir in butter, lemon peel and juice. Pour into pastry shell and bake for approximately 30 minutes in a 350 degree oven. Protect crust edges with foil, if necessary, so as not to brown too quickly.

MERINGUE:
6 egg whites at room temperature
1 teaspoon vanilla
1/2 teaspoon cream of tartar
12 Tablespoons sugar

Beat egg whites until they begin to form peaks. Add vanilla and cream of tartar and continue to beat to soft peaks. Gradually add sugar, 1 tablespoon at a time, continuing to beat for about 5 minutes or until peaks are high, stiff and glossy. Mound meringue on lemon filling and seal meringue to crust. Bake about 15 minutes until meringue is golden. Cool at room temperature. Refrigerate for another 1 1/2 hours before slicing to serve.

Fudgey Pecan Pie

Diane M. waited many months before the recipe she had once clipped from the Wisconsin State Journal and baked for her family was again made available to her, this time from three faithful readers.

1/3 cup butter or margarine
2/3 cup sugar
1/3 cup cocoa
3 eggs
1 cup light corn syrup
1/4 teaspoon salt
1 cup chopped pecans
1 unbaked 9-inch pie crust
Sweetened whipped cream (see note)
Pecan halves, optional

Heat oven to 375 degrees. In medium saucepan over low heat, melt butter. Add sugar and cocoa, stirring until well blended. Remove from heat; set aside. In medium bowl, beat eggs lightly. Stir in corn syrup and salt. Add cocoa mixture; blend well. Stir in chopped pecans. Pour into unbaked pie crust. Bake for 45 to 50 minutes or until set. Cool. Cover, let stand 8 hours before serving. Garnish with sweetened whipped cream and pecan halves, if desired. Note: To sweeten whipped cream, stir together 1/2 cup cold whipped cream, 1 tablespoon powdered sugar and 1/4 teaspoon vanilla extract; beat until stiff.

Makes about 1 cup.

CRUST

STIR-N-ROLL PASTRY (DOUBLE CRUST)
2 cups sifted all-purpose flour
1 1/2 teaspoons salt
1/2 cup Wesson oil
1/4 cup cold whole milk
Heat oven as directed in pie filling recipe. Mix flour and salt. Pour Wesson oil and milk into one measuring cup (but don't stir); add all at once to flour. Stir until mixed. Press into smooth ball. Cut in halves; flatten slightly.

BOTTOM CRUST:
Place half between 2 sheets of waxed paper (12 inches square). Dampen table top to prevent slipping. Roll out gently to edges of paper. Peel off top paper. If dough tears, mend without moistening. Place paper side up in 8- or 9-inch pie pan. Peel off paper. Ease and fit pastry into pan. Trim even with rim. Add filling.

TOP CRUST:
Roll as above and place over filling. Fold edges under bottom crust. Seal by pressing gently with fork or by fluting edge. Snip 3 or 4 small slits near center for steam to escape. Bake as directed in filling recipe.

STIR-N-ROLL PASTRY (SINGLE CRUST):
1 1/3 cups sifted all-purpose flour
1 teaspoon salt
1/3 cup Wesson oil
3 Tablespoons cold whole milk
Heat oven to 475 degrees or as directed in pie filling recipe. Follow directions for double crust pie. Fit carefully into pie pan. Flute edge. Prick thoroughly with fork. Bake 8 to 10 minutes. Cool. Add filling. In some pies, filling and crust are baked together. Do not prick pastry before filling.

ICE WATER PIE CRUST:
2 cups flour
1/2 cup cooking oil
5 Tablespoons ice water
It is not necessary to sift flour. Place in large mixing bowl and make a well in center. Pour oil in center. Add

ice water. Stir to blend until it forms a ball. Divide into 2 sections. Roll each section between waxed paper. For a 10-inch double crust, increase proportions to 3 cups of flour, 3/4 cup cooking oil and 7 tablespoons ice water.

CRISCO PAT-A-PIE

2 cups flour

1 1/2 teaspoons salt

2 teaspoons sugar

2/3 cup Crisco oil

3 Tablespoons milk

Sift flour, salt and sugar into an 8- or 9-inch pie pan. Mix milk into Crisco oil and add to dry mixture. Continue mixing until all dry ingredients are damp. Reserve 1/3 of mixture for top. Press the 2/3 of dough evenly around sides and bottom of pie pan. Fill with fruit filling and crumble remainder of dough on top. Bake according to the pie recipe you are using.

NEVER FAIL PIE CRUST (Island City Cafe, Cumberland):

3 cups flour

1 teaspoon salt

1 1/4 cups shortening (butter or plain solid Crisco)

1 egg

1 teaspoon vinegar

5 1/2 Tablespoons cold water

Mix flour, salt and shortening with pastry blender until blended. Mix egg, vinegar and water together and add to flour mixture. Stir with fork until crust forms a ball. Divide into four balls.

Makes 2 double pies, or 4 single crusts.

MERINGUE:

6 egg whites at room temperature

1 teaspoon vanilla

1/2 teaspoon cream of tartar

12 Tablespoons sugar

Beat egg whites until they begin to form peaks. Add vanilla and cream of tartar and continue to beat to soft peaks. Gradually add sugar, 1 tablespoon at a time, continuing to beat for about 5 minutes or until peaks are high, stiff and glossy. Mound meringue on lemon filling and seal meringue to crust. Bake about 15 minutes until meringue is golden. Cool at room temperature. Refrigerate for another 1 1/2 hours before slicing to serve.

NEVER FAIL PIE CRUST:

3 cups all-purpose flour

1 teaspoon salt

1 1/4 cup shortening

1 egg beaten

5 Tablespoons cold water

1 Tablespoon vinegar

In large bowl, mix flour and salt. Using a pastry blender, cut in shortening until well-blended. In a l-cup liquid measure, combine egg, water and vinegar. Add all at once to flour mxiture, blending with a spoon or fork until flour is moistened. Divide evenly in 3 pieces. Pat out l piece on a lightly floured surface or between 2 pieces waxed paper. Using a lightly floured rolling pin, roll dough to a l0-inch circle. Carefully transfer to an 8-inch pie plate. Repeat with remaining dough or wrap in plastic wrap and refrigerate up to 2 weeks or freeze. Makes pastry for l two-crust 8-inch pie and l single crust pie. Recipe from "America's Best Blue Ribbon Winning State Fair Recipes," by Catherine Hanley.

In 1889, Elva and Mary Bryant, the
Attic Angel inspiration, were
instrumental in starting our legacy.

Lunch with
the ladies

. . . . ●

YEARS AGO, MANY HOMES WERE BUILT WITH WALKUP ATTICS. REACHED BY A NARROW STAIRCASE, EACH ATTIC HAD ITS OWN WAY OF EMBRACING THE PAST WITH ITEMS LACED WITH SENTIMENT, OR THOSE DEEMED TOO VALUABLE TO DISCARD. Lacking insulation, attics were bitter cold during winter months and, in the heat of summer, unbearably stuffy. Naked floor boards squeaked with each step; the only light that pierced the dusty stillness snuck through a lone window pane on bright sunny days. Yet, despite the seemingly unhealthy conditions, an elegance often prevailed.

It was in such an attic 106 years ago that Gen. E. E. Bryant's daughters spent playtime with friends during spring and fall. Fascinated with what was stored in their room at the top, they wiled away countless hours exploring family treasures. Clothing, once worn with pride, hung from hangers hooked over heavy nails in wooden beams. High-button shoes that had moved with gracefulness stood alone on a shelf. Messages of life, and love, were neatly tied with satin ribbons and tucked beneath finery folded and laid to rest in the old family trunk. Other clothing, slightly outdated and no longer wearable, was packed in boxes. Elva and Mary Bryant, who were lovingly referred to by their father as "attic angels," heard one day about a family in need. Compassion sent them to the attic; they descended hours later carrying bundles of clothing. Thus was the innocent beginning of the Attic Angels, a nonprofit group that is recognized today as the oldest philanthropic organization in Wisconsin. However social their initial meetings were, Elva, Mary and 14 others approached each community need with concern. When they realized that they, too, needed help to carry on their work, fund-raisers with cookbooks and charity balls

• were planned. Major statements within the community began in 1902 when the Attic Angel Association gave $1,000 to the Madison General Hospital Association as a first pledge toward the building of their hospital. In 1908, Attic Angels brought the first visiting nurse to Madison. Child health care centers were followed by a seemingly endless list of helping hands that embraced the city, just as they do today. With members and volunteers offering an excess of 35,000 hours of service annually, their primary focus is the 70-unit Attic Angel Tower, a retirement home for the elderly, and the adjacent nursing home. One of their most successful fund-raisers has been their annual House and Garden Tour and Luncheon.

Attic Angel Macaroni Salad

When Irene Capossela wrote to me about the macaroni salad the Attic Angels served for years at their annual fund-raising luncheons, after contacting longtime "Angel" Marian Dean, the group gave its permission to share the recipe with Capossela and thousands of others who remember it with great fondness.

1 cup mayonnaise

2 1/2 ounces Durkee sauce

2 cups diced ham

3 cups small shell macaroni, cooked

2 1/2 cups chopped celery

1/2 of a 4-ounce jar of sweet relish

3 eggs, chopped

1/8 cup chopped, stuffed olives

1 cup diced Cheddar cheese

One 10-ounce jar of tiny peas, drained

Combine mayonnaise and Durkee sauce and fold into other ingredients, adding peas last.

Serves 12 small portions.

Note: This was served on a lettuce leaf with a small bunch of red grapes, slices of cheese, and an assortment of sweet breads and bars.

Attic Angel Zucchini Bread

Served for many years with Attic Angel summer luncheons.

3 eggs
2 cups sugar
1 cup oil
1 Tablespoon vanilla
3 cups grated zucchini, drained
3 cups flour
1 teaspoon salt
1 teaspoon baking soda
1/2 teaspoon baking powder
1 Tablespoon cinnamon
1 cup chopped nuts or raisins

Beat eggs until light and fluffy. Slowly add sugar; add oil and vanilla. Add well-drained zucchini. Mix dry ingredients and add to mixture, adding nuts or raisins last. Bake in 2 greased 9x5x3-inch loaf pans for 1 hour at 325 degrees. Check after 40 minutes for doneness.

Blueberry Brunch Bread–
Signature Room at the 95th

Owners Rick Roman and Nick Pyknis serve this bread during their Sunday brunch in the upscale restaurant in the John Hancock Center on North Michigan Avenue in Chicago. Jill Cook, who initially requested the recipe, now can prepare it in her own kitchen in Pardeeville.

8 ounces cream cheese

1 cup butter

1 1/2 cup sugar

4 eggs; juice and zest of 1 lemon

1 Tablespoon vanilla

1/2 cup flour

1 Tablespoon baking powder

1 teaspoon salt

2 cups fresh blueberries, or frozen, unthawed

Mix cheese, butter, sugar and eggs; add juice and zest of lemon and vanilla to cheese mixture. Mix low speed for 1 minute. Do not over mix. Add berries and fold carefully into mixture. Bake in dusted or Pam-sprayed paper lined loaf pans in a 350 degree oven for 45 minutes or until tested done.

Hyatt Regency Grand Cypress' Three Melon Soup

Nancy Urso returned from a Caribbean cruise in love with a melon soup. This recipe was found in "A Taste of Florida" cookbook compiled by retired Orlando Sentinel Food Editor Dorothy Chapman.

As a favorite recipe served at the Florida hotel, I had hoped it was close to what Urso remembered from her trip

5 whole cantaloupe melons, divided
1 whole honeydew melon
3/4 cup watermelon chunks,
seeds removed
Three 6-ounce containers plain yogurt
1 ounce Coco Lopez cream of coconut
1 ounce white wine
1 ounce Midori melon liqueur
Salt to taste
Juice of lemon
8 whole fresh strawberries
Mint leaves

Use 3 of the cantaloupes for make 6 serving bowls by cutting them in half. Scoop out seeds and trim the rim of each melon bowl leaving 1-inch of meat on the perimeter; set aside. Halve remaining cantaloupe and honeydew melons; discard seeds and scoop out meat in chunks. Place fruit in blender container or food processor and blend at high speed until pureed. Strain. Blend in yogurt.

Bacon, Lettuce and Tomato Soup– The Past & Present Inn, Cross Plains

Cross Plains is a short drive from Madison and a must for those who appreciate a delicious taste of yesteryear. The inn, located on Highway 14 that passes through town, has an array of small rooms on the first floor that offer visitors a shopping experience after they dine.

1/2 cup margarine
2/3 cup flour
1 quart milk
2 cups chicken stock
10 slices crisp-fried bacon, crumbled
1 cup lettuce, finely chopped
1/2 cup tomato, finely chopped
2 Tablespoons white Worcestershire
1/2 teaspoon nutmeg
1/4 teaspoon pepper
1/4 teaspoon Italian seasoning (optional)

Melt margarine, blend in flour. Add milk, cook and stir until thickened. Bring chicken stock to a boil and add bacon and vegetables. Continue cooking to heat vegetables.

Combine stock mixture with cream soup. Season.

COLD LEMON CHICKEN SALAD

Past issues of Bon Appetit were tied in bundles to place (reluctantly) at the curb when Diana Erfurth called to tell me about the salad recipe from 1980 that she had misplaced. I rescued the correct bundle just in time, then managed to find a spot on a garage shelf to hide them once again.

3 to 3 1/2-pound whole chicken

3 cups water

1/2 onion

1 carrot

1 garlic clove

Parsley sprigs

Salt and freshly ground pepper to taste

2 cups fresh bean sprouts

Boiling water

2 eggs, beaten

LEMON DRESSING:

1 cup broth from chicken

2 Tablespoons sugar or to taste

1 teaspoon cornstarch

Finely grated peel and juice of 3 lemons

Salt and freshly ground white pepper

2 cups drained canned bamboo shoots, shredded

2 green onions, thinly sliced

2 lemons, halved lengthwise and cut into thin half-moon slices

Combine first 6 ingredients with salt and pepper in large saucepan. Cover and bring to boil; reduce heat and simmer until cooked through, about 45 minutes. Remove chicken and set aside to cool. Strain broth, reserving 1 cup for dressing. Discard skin and bones from chicken; shred meat and set aside. Place bean sprouts in colander and pour boiling water over; rinse quickly in cold water and drain well. Pour eggs into 8-inch pan and make thin omelet. Turn out of pan, cool slightly and cut into shreds. Combine all ingredients for dressing in small saucepan and simmer over low heat, stirring frequently, until slightly thickened. Set aside to cool. Combine chicken,

bean sprouts, omelet, dressing and bamboo shoots in
large bowl and toss thoroughly. Arrange in center of
platter. Sprinkle with onion and surround with lemon
slices.

Serves 4.

HALLE'S FAMOUS ALMOND RAREBIT

Welsh rarebit served for years at Halle's department store dining room in Cleveland, Ohio, and enjoyed by reader Barbara Price, Fitchburg.

4 Tablespoons butter
4 Tablespoons flour
1/2 teaspoon dry mustard
1 teaspoon salt
1/4 teaspoon paprika
1 cup milk
1 cup cream
Drop of Tabasco sauce
1 Tablespoon Worcestershire sauce
1/2 pound sharp Cheddar cheese, grated
Melba toast
Whole almonds, toasted

Melt butter in top of double boiler and stir in flour with next three ingredients. Stir in milk and cream slowly until smooth and thickened. Add Tabasco sauce, Worcestershire sauce and cheese. Stir until lumps disappear. Pour over crisscrossed melba toast. Sprinkle generously with unbuttered, unsalted toasted blanched almonds.

Serves 5.

STUFFED BAKED POTATO SUPERB

Easy to prepare with an endless list of ways to change the ingredients and flavors for a delicate or hearty touch. It was found in a fundraising cookbook titled Camp HOPE, submitted in memory of Adam Moore who died of cancer in 1969, just shy of his fifth birthday.

2 baked potatoes
1 can cream of broccoli cheese soup
One (16-ounce) bag of frozen broccoli and cauliflower, cooked
1 small onion, minced, optional
Small amount of milk
Cooked ham or other meat, optional

Cut a deep slice lengthwise into the baked potatoes. Set aside. In a saucepan warm the soup and add milk to get to desired consistency. Stir in cooked vegetables and meat.

Heat until warm. Serve hot over the cut baked potatoes.
Makes two to four servings.

STRAWBERRY BUTTER

A request was made for the strawberry butter served at a Brookfield hotel. The chef wouldn't part with the recipe so I let my fingers do a little walking, all the way to Manhatten in New York City and Sheila Lukins' and Julee Rosso's successful Silver Palate gourmet shop.

8 Tablespoons (1 stick) sweet butter
1/3 cup strawberry jam
1/2 teaspoon fresh lemon juice
1/2 teaspoon confectioners' sugar

Cream ingredients together, transfer to a small crock and chill. The butter will keep several days in the refrigerator or many weeks in the freezer. Let butter return to room temperature before serving.

Schaum Torte– Otto's Inn, Watertown

When I think of bridge luncheons, I also think of delicious desserts. This recipe was passed on to Joyce Deily's mother many years ago by the staff at Otto's Inn. It is light, beautiful and worthy of the time to make it.

6 egg whites

2 cups sugar

1/2 teaspoon cream of tartar

1/2 teaspoon baking powder

1 teaspoon vanilla

Sweetened fresh strawberries or other fresh sweetened fruit

Heavy cream, whipped, or ice cream

With an electric mixer, beat all ingredients except strawberries and whipped cream for 1 hour. Bake approximately 1 hour at 200 degrees. Serve strawberries over each serving and top with whipped cream.

Note: This was baked in a pan and cut into squares, rather than being dropped by spoonfuls, as most schaum torte recipes suggest. Deily's mother used a glass, 7-1/2-x12-inch pan. Although this recipe doesn't mention preparing the glass pan, I have a baked meringue recipe that requires buttering the pan before pouring in the meringue to bake.

Grandpa and Grandma Kovacs
and me – 1940.

Summer
gardens

· •

My Hungarian-born grandfather, Joe Kovacs, was the groundskeeper of Tenney Park for many years. Manicured conditions throughout the park showed his deep respect for the land he tended and the lagoons that wove an endless path of shallow water under weeping willows and wood and stone bridges. On days off, he rode the waves of Lake Mendota in a small wooden flat-bottom boat, catching fish so large that they dragged behind him when he walked home for supper. Residents of Marston Avenue loved Grandpa and often asked his advice for problems or possibilities that surfaced in their own yards and gardens. With immigrant pride and a heavy accent, he would share what he had learned from years of experience.

On the corner of North Thornton Avenue and East Johnson Street was Grandpa's tool shed – a small wooden shack with a stool inside to sit on while he ate the lunch he carried from home in a black lunch bucket. Sometimes I would join him with my own sandwich, and once my sister walked there with Grandma to deliver a dish of freshly made Hungarian goulash. But, otherwise, he ate alone, staring out at traffic through a makeshift open shutter, or to the left at the Yahara River. Following the river to Sherman Avenue and across the bridge to the north was the old malt house owned by Hausmann Brewery. Between the malt house, where a branch of CUNA is today, and the length of the river, was Grandpa's garden. No ordinary garden, but instead a bona fide Victory Garden, to grow food for Grandma to preserve for their meals during World War II.

He was well into his 60s then, and each spring, in shirt sleeves and a straw hat, Grandpa would turn over the earth for planting seeds, and the spading, weeding, watering, hoeing, and finally, harvesting that would follow. Gardening today has reached the ultimate in popularity as watching something grow, then nourishing it along the way, becomes not only therapeutic, but also healthy and delicious. Grandpa would be in awe of the offerings at the Farmers' Market, fully appreciating the efforts of so many that develop into delectable rewards for others.

STRAWBERRY FRUIT SOUP

Grandma Kovacs was an excellent cook who combined on a daily basis the flavors of Grandpa's birthplace in Hungary, and Germany where she was born. Although both countries are known for their cold fruit soups, I doubt that was what Grandpa had in mind when he picked juicy red strawberries in the noon day sun. Chef LaMonte Johnson, who learned to cook in his grandmother's Creole kitchen in New Orleans, prepares this recipe at the Hilton Hotel and Convention Center in Oshkosh.

    1 pint well-creamed strawberries
    1/4 cup Rose's lime juice
    1/4 cup Amaretto di Saronno
    1/3 cup granulated sugar (varies with sweetness of berries)
    1 pint sour cream
    1 pint heavy cream (if this amount does not fit, reserve some to add later)
    Dash of nutmeg, preferably freshly grated

In large blender, assemble ingredients. Blend until texture is smooth and all the sour cream has been incorporated. Feel free to add more of any ingredient to suit your taste. Serve chilled.

Note: Any brand of Amaretto can be used, however, Johnson recommends substitutions only "in a pinch." Strawberry soup can be served in many different ways. Left overnight, the thick cream can be used as a strawberry creme fraiche, or with additional amaretto poured into chocolate cups for a tasty holiday cordial, but best served on its own with, perhaps, a butter cookie.

Boorsma Crock Dill Pickles

When Steven Keip contacted me about pickles soaked in brine with garlic and dill, many favorite pickle recipes arrived from the good cooks of Wisconsin. It was difficult to make selections, but when I read about the pickles made in Jo Ann Winzenried's kitchen in Monticello, and how everyone expects "Winzenried pickles" at potlucks, and about the gallon jar her daughter took to a Super Bowl party, I decided it had to be a winner.

1 cup pickling salt
3 cups vinegar
9 cups water
50 medium, freshly picked cucumbers
Fresh dill
Garlic cloves
Small lump of alum, if desired

Combine salt, vinegar and water and heat to boiling; set aside. Sterilize a 6-gallon crock. Prick cucumbers with fork. Fill crock, alternating cucumbers with layer of dill and garlic cloves. Top with a few pieces of lump alum, if desired. Fill crock to overflowing with warm brine. Cover with stone plate, weighing it to keep cucumbers under brine. Let stand in a warm place up to 3 days or until dilled as desired. Refrigerate.

EASIEST EVER BREAD AND BUTTER PICKLES

Emily Knoche clipped this recipe from the Sawyer County Record in Hayward and described the pickles as "delicious."

1 quart jar no-garlic dill pickles
1/3 cup vinegar,
1 1/2 cup sugar
1 teaspoon celery seed
1 teaspoon mustard seed.

Drain juice from quart of dill pickles. Discard juice. Slice pickles into rounds. Put sliced pickles and other ingredients back into jar. Shake a few times to blend all. Put cover on and let sit in refrigerator for about a week.

Note: Emily Knoche clipped this recipe from the Sawyer County Record in Hayward and calls the pickles "fabulous."

Nita's Candied Pickle Strips

Made and served at the Skunk's Nest Restaurant in Wildwood, Florida, these can be prepared with the cheapest brand of dill pickles with garlic, as suggested by Kathryn Fell.

1/2 gallon whole dill pickles
2 cups sugar
1/2 cup vinegar
1/4 cup water
1 teaspoon pickling spice

Wash pickles in cold water; dry thoroughly. Cut in strips. Bring sugar, vinegar, water and spices to boil. Let cool. Pour over pickles packed in jars that have tight lids. Turn upside down for 3 days while storing in the refrigerator.

Freezer Mock Raspberry Jam

This green tomato jam was made and served at an autumn church retreat for young teenage confirmands.

Many who turned up their noses at the bounty of tomato dishes served that morning for breakfast were wild over this. They never guessed it, too, contained tomatoes . . . the unripe kind.

4 cups chopped, ground or pureed green tomatoes

4 cups granulated sugar

One 6-ounce package raspberry flavored gelatin

Puree or finely grind tomatoes in food grinder, blender, or food processor. Add sugar. Mix well. Bring to a boil, stirring. Add gelatin, stir to mix. Simmer for 20 minutes. Remove from heat. Ladle hot mixture into sterilized containers. Refrigerate for use within one week. Freeze for longer storage.

PRISCILLA'S RASPBERRY JAM

This was a surprise for me. Raspberry jam made with green tomatoes? Naomi Rockwell, Oregon, just happened to have the recipe customers enjoy at Priscilla's Restaurant in Bunkport, Maine.

4 cups ground green tomatoes (drain most of juice)

4 cups sugar

1 large package raspberry flavored gelatin

Mix together and bring to a boil. Boil over medium heat for 4 minutes. Pour into prepared jars and seal. This can also be frozen. It spreads better if not refrigerated after being opened.

Makes about 6 jars of jam.

FRESH TOMATO-BASIL SAUCE

Preparing authentic spaghetti sauce doesn't have to take two hours to stir and simmer. This quick and delicious recipe comes from a cookbook that says it all. "Cucina Paradiso, The Heavenly Food of Sicily."

2 garlic cloves, peeled and slightly crushed
4 Tablespoons olive oil
1 medium onion, finely chopped
2 pounds tomatoes, peeled, seeded, and finely chopped
6 fresh basil leaves
Salt and pepper

Saute garlic in olive oil in deep saute pan until it turns golden. Remove and discard garlic and add onion. Cook onion until translucent. Add tomatoes with their liquid, the basil, and salt and pepper to taste. Cook on high heat for 20 to 25 minutes, uncovered. When sauce is finished, turn heat off, and allow to steep for 10 minutes before serving.

Makes 2 to 3 cups.

Note: Some dried oregano can be added, if desired, when sauce is finished and heat has been turned off to steep. Also, to peel whole tomatoes, lower in boiling water for 30 seconds or so until skins slip off easily.

SEASONED TOMATO AND ONION SALAD

This was one of the first requests that appeared in my column, Cooks' Exchange. When Barbara Schweich's letter arrived, I knew it had to be the same recipe submitted by Mrs. Charles Mobray, Janesville, for the 1973 Wisconsin State Journal cookbook. It gained their recognition and became one of my favorites, too.

1 teaspoon salt
1 teaspoon ground basil
1/2 teaspoon sugar
1/2 teaspoon dill
1/8 teaspoon freshly ground pepper
4 large tomatoes, sliced 1/4 inch thick
4 thin slices Spanish onion, separated into rings
Romaine or other lettuce leaves

Mix salt, basil, sugar, dill and pepper.

Place one-fourth of tomatoes and onion rings in 10x6x1 1/2-inch baking dish. Sprinkle with one-fourth of the herb mixture. Repeat layers three times. Cover. Refrigerate three to four hours. To serve, arrange tomatoes and onions on lettuce leaves. Spoon some of the liquid over tomatoes.

Serves 6 to 8.

Salsa

The responses from readers for salsa recipes were as plentiful as a warm fall harvest. And although each recipe was somewhat different, most came with the recommendation to use the seeds and pith of jalapeno peppers if hot salsa was desired; otherwise, for a medium hot recipe, remove only half of the seeds. This recipe makes a small amount and is perfect for someone who is experimenting in the preparation of salsa for the first time.

    1 small onion, finely chopped
    2 garlic cloves, finely chopped
    3 large tomatoes, peeled and finely chopped
    2 to 4 jalapeno peppers, seeded and diced
    1/4 cup minced cilantro
    1/2 teaspoon salt
    1 Tablespoon fresh lime juice

In a small bowl, combine onion and garlic. Pour enough boiling water over to cover. Let stand two minutes and drain. Add tomatoes, jalapeno peppers, lime juice and cilantro. Taste and add salt as needed.

Ghafoor Zafari, owner Kabul Restaurant.

Local restaurant secrets

· ●

STATE STREET. . . THAT GREAT STREET. LYRICS TO THE SONG ABOUT THE MAGNIFICENT STRIP IN THE WINDY CITY COULD EASILY DESCRIBE OUR VERY OWN STATE STREET IN MADISON. Making a connection between the Capitol Square and UW-Madison, State Street's seven blocks have offered just about everything. My own recollections, vivid, yet limited, begin as a child in the 1940s, later as a student, then a taxpaying adult, and many years later, once again a student. It takes but a second to trigger one's mind when thinking back on the many phases of State Street and mine usually ends up absorbed in the category of food.

It seems to follow a pattern that starts with the Hot Fudge Mary Janes served at Rennebohm's Drug Store in the second block of State Street. I remember the hot roast beef sandwiches next door at the Spanish Cafe and the delicious homemade rhubarb pie served at Weber's Restaurant a few buildings further. Hugging the west wall of the Orpheum Theatre, Weber's ran the width of State to East Johnson street with a long counter and a seemingly endless string of booths. At the end of the block in one of the many tiny triangular shops beginning and ending each block was the Caramel Crisp Shop and the best caramel corn in the world. There were two Greek-owned restaurants in the third block. One, a gathering place for Central High students, was called George's (Gerothanas), and, next door, was Notes' family-owned Coney Island, where wieners visible in the front window were heated on a stainless steel machine and carried in a Ferris wheel motion until removed, placed in a bun and smothered with their famous chili sauce. One could never forget the Chocolate Shop two blocks down where hand-dipped chocolates were tiered and protected in glass showcases surrounded by polished heavy dark wood panels that glowed from ornate light fixtures guiding customers to the mezzanine, today offering treasures from the Far East in Fritz Ragatz's Oriental Specialties Shop, back then to high-backed wood booths where I devoured my first Swiss Miss hot milk sundae, never to be forgotten. Down another block and across the street, Matt Lombardino's Italian Village served homemade pizza to teen-agers in cozy booths, and Italian dinners to adults seated at white wrought-iron furniture in an adjoining room in the ambience of the country Lombardino left behind. Loved family members share stories of their many weekly after-work visits in the 1920s to a Chinese restaurant serving Cantonese extra-fine chop suey and egg foo yung, while Frances Lee, 84, of Darlington, recently described the coleslaw made daily in the 1930s at Giller's Delicatessen. The list goes on and on. State Street has been a virtual menu of ethnic diversity - melting pot appeal - past, present, and, hopefully, forever future. To nourish my education of the exciting tastes of this great street, a request arrived from Lisa Pena for Mashawa Soup, a house specialty at Kabul Restaurant, 541 State St. Pena moved out of state and "hated" thinking she may never taste the soup again. A short time later, another request for the same soup arrived from Helen Phelps and Deb Haines. I decided to see for myself and, once again, came home smiling. Ghafoor and Saboor Zafari opened Wisconsin's first Afghanistan restaurant in 1987, and Madison's first in 1990. The location was - where else? - State Street, across the curbs and two blocks down from the Second Story, a restaurant featuring French cuisine, purchased by the Zafaris in 1938. Kabul, with its Mediterranean flavors, was immediately responded to by those forever in search of another exceptional and unique eating spot. Rightfully proud of their roots, the country and the nostalgic attachment to their food, Ghafoor is quick to point out that Afghani food is delightfully spicy but not hot. At Kabul, spices and herbs are ground daily for freshness. Although rice, couscous, breads and soups are basic items in Afghanistan, the menu also includes vegetarian, lamb, beef and chicken dishes prepared from family recipes and those shared by friends. Fresh blue marlin, salmon, swordfish and other seafood appear alternately as daily specials to balance an intriguing selection.

MASHAWA SOUP

State Street, that great Street. The area continues to enthrall Madisonians, students and visitors with a myriad of flavors. At Kabul restaurant, I was treated to a memorable lunch in a bowl of flavors never before savored. Served, also, was the recipe owner Ghafoor Zafari was so kind to share with me for a reader who was leaving town and couldn't bear the thought of never again tasting mashawa soup.

1 large onion, diced
8 ounces chopped lamb (leg of lamb, fatless)
8 ounces chopped chicken breast
1 cup dry garbanzo beans
1 cup dry light kidney beans
1/2 cup green split peas
1/2 cup yellow split peas
2 Tablespoons crushed tomatoes
1 Tablespoon salt
1 Tablespoon dill weed
3/4 Tablespoon cayenne pepper
1/2 Tablespoon black pepper
1/2 Tablespoon dried cilantro
2 ounces chicken stock
1 cup cooked rice

Brown onion in vegetable oil, add lamb and chicken and saute. In separate kettle, put all beans and peas, cover with water and boil for one hour. In the lamb and chicken mixture add the remaining ingredients except the rice, then add 1/2 gallon of water. Bring to boil, simmer for 2 hours. When finished, pour both mixtures together. Add rice.

Note: Garnish mashawa soup with a tablespoon of yogurt sauce, and serve with Afghani flat bread .

YOGURT SAUCE:
8 ounces plain yogurt
2 cloves garlic, crushed
1 teaspoon ground mint.

Mix together ingredients. Put a tablespoon of yogurt sauce on each soup serving.

Governor's Pork (or Lamb)– Imperial Gardens, Middleton

There was a time when Madison had few Cantonese restaurants to satisfy our cravings for authentic Oriental food. Today we are blessed with many that offer a variety of regional foods from China, and Japan as well. The Imperial Gardens in Middleton is located on the busy corner of University Avenue and Allen Boulevard. The decor is exquisite, and each menu item exquisitely delicious. Taiwanese-born owners Henry and Fei Chen have shared their knowledge of prize-winning Chinese food with Madisonians since 1974 and were happy to divulge their secrets for a favorite menu item requested by Patty Pieper, Dalton, However once again, I must caution you that trying to duplicate the same quality in your own kitchen is difficult because we lack the equipment necessary for high the temperatures imperative to authenticity. But then, it's always fun to try...

12 ounces thinly sliced pork or lamb
1 ounce cornstarch
1 egg
10 ounces oil (for deep drying)
1 ounce vegetable oil
1/2 ounce minced garlic
7 hot peppers
1 ounce chopped scallions
2 ounces sliced bamboo shoots
2 ounces cut broccoli, optional
2 1/2 teaspoons soy sauce
1 1/2 teaspoons sugar
Touch of dry white wine
2 to 3 teaspoons cornstarch/water mixture
Dry roasted peanuts, optional
Touch of sesame oil

Mix a half egg and 1 ounce cornstarch with sliced pork. Deep fry the pork in hot oil. Set aside. Preheat the wok. Heat 1 ounce vegetable oil. Add garlic, red peppers and scallions. Stir. Add pork, bamboo shoots and broccoli.

Stir fry together for approximately one minute. Add soy
sauce and sugar. Add a touch of white wine. Then add 2
to 3 teaspoons cornstarch mixed with water. Finally, add
peanuts, if desired and a touch of sesame oil.

   Note: All ingredients can be adjusted to taste.

MANDARIN-STYLE GOVERNOR'S CHICKEN— IMPERIAL PALACE

Bobby and Jenny Lee welcomed me into their kitchen with open arms so that I could watch carefully how orders are prepared in their N. Sherman Avenue restaurant. The Lees and their trained crew of cooks work like computers. No cookbooks are in sight so I became the one with a clipboard and pencil to jot down what I thought to be the correct measurements for this recipe. Let's face it folks. Unless you have a Danny Kaye kitchen (Kaye was known for having an authentic Oriental kitchen installed in his home), it will be nearly impossible to reproduce authentically. Besides, the ambiance of the Imperial Palace makes you feel like royalty. The Lees were proud to share the recipe requested as the favorite of many readers.

  2 chicken thighs and legs, or two chicken breasts
  boned and skinned
  1 whole egg, slightly beaten
  2 to 3 Tablespoons cornstarch
  1 to 2 Tablespoons vegetable oil
  10 dried red pepper pods for a mildly hot flavor
  1/2 cup diagonally sliced scallions, about 2 inches in
  length, using both white and green parts
  1 cup sliced drained water chestnuts
  1 teaspoon minced garlic
  1 teaspoon cooking wine
  3 to 4 Tablespoons soy sauce
  2 Tablespoons sugar
  2 Tablespoons chicken broth
  1 teaspoon cornstarch mixed with small amount of cold
  water
  1/2 to 1 teaspoon sesame oil
  Deep-fried skinless peanuts
  Steamed white rice
Uniformly cube meat to resemble the size of pineapple chunks. Dredge in beaten egg to coat thoroughly, then dust with cornstarch, shaking off excess. Bring oil to high

heat in wok and stir-fry quickly, about 1 to 2 minutes, until chicken is thoroughly cooked. Carefully remove from pan and set aside, reserving oil in pan. Stir-fry dried red pepper pods until one side is dark and the other side remains red. Do not darken too much or the flavor will become bitter. Add scallions and water chestnuts to wok and stir-fry about 30 seconds. Add garlic, cooking wine, soy sauce, sugar and broth to vegetables and return chicken to mixture, cooking together quickly for a few minutes. Add the cornstarch-water mixture and stir into pan to thicken juices. Add 1/2 teaspoon sesame oil and stir to flavor. Add peanuts that have been deep-fried until crispy and lightly golden in color. Serve with hot white rice.

Makes 1 to 2 servings.

Chocolate Steamed Pudding— Kennedy Manor Dining Room and Bar

Thank goodness, developers have not erased the ambiance of Langdon Street for it is with the entry to the east and the Kennedy Manor that the past begins. Call it a priceless gem, a crown jewel, or a family treasure. Whatever description you choose, Kennedy Manor has retained the timelessness that Madisonians should bow to. Andrea Craig and Nancy Christy are its polished owners, fine tuning everything they set out to do. Because of this talented duo, the lower level dining room has once again been placed on a pedestal by those with exquisite taste who visit the restaurant time and time again.

9 ounces bittersweet chocolate
6 ounces unsalted butter
6 eggs, separated
1 cup granulated white sugar
1/4 cup all-purpose flour

Combine chocolate and butter in bowl over a water bath/double boiler and melt slowly over low-simmering water. When melted, thoroughly combine and pull off the heat. In a separate bowl beat the egg whites on high speed until foamy, add 1/2 cup sugar and continue to beat the whites until soft peaks form and hold. Remove bowl from mixer and put aside. In a third bowl, beat the egg yolks on high and slowly add remaining 1/2 cup sugar. Continue to beat until the volume triples, the color is light yellow and the sugar has dissolved. Add the melted chocolate/butter mixture and beat until thoroughly blended. Add flour to mixture and beat on low to blend, then beat on high for 10 seconds. Turn the mixer down to low again and begin to add the already beaten egg whites to the chocolate mixture. Combine thoroughly. Stop the mixer, detach the bowl and scrape along the sides and bottom of the bowl to make sure that you have incorporated all of the chocolate. This mixture can be stored in the refrigerator at this point for two days, or baked immediately in individual heat-resistant custard cups, or in one 9-inch cake pan. Fill the cups or pan to the rim and level. Place the cake inside a roasting pan or larger cake pan. Fill this larger pan with 1 inch warm water. Cover and seal with metal foil (allowing 2 inches above cake to rise). Either place on the stovetop on medium-high heat until you hear the water boiling, then turn heat to low for 30 minutes or place in 325 degree oven for 45 minutes. Be careful on the stovetop not to let the water boil away. Add more water as needed or turn your temperature down. While cooking, the cake will swell and expand 1 to 2 inches above the rim, but will deflate upon cooling. Loosen the cake around the edge with a knife and invert onto plate to serve. Serve with fresh vanilla ice cream and your favorite chocolate sauce. Garnish with mint.

Jumpin' Jamaican Jerk Salad- Milan's, Whitney Way

This is Mike Brusca's newest take-out or eat-in location in Madison. Planted with ancestral Sicilian seeds, the choices found on the menu include the new wave of Caribbean Island flavors everyone is talking about. You may need to visually search the block, but the restaurant is there, at 628 S. Whitney Way, hidden behind a large franchise restaurant near the busy corner of Whitney Way and Odana. A cafeteria-style line is waiting beyond the front door, where smiling faces of employees are waiting to prepare, as you like, orders from the menu. The jerk salad is just one of many to please adventuresome cravings.

2 whole chicken breasts (4 single breasts), skinned
1 cup jerk seasoning (see note)
2 ripe mangoes
1 ounce olive oil, plus enough extra for rubbing on vegetables before cooking
2 ounces sesame seeds
2 large red bell peppers
One (16-ounce can) pineapple rings, drained, saving juice
1 fresh fennel bulb
4 ounces coarsely chopped walnuts
8 ounces pineapple juice

Prepare seasoning according to instructions. Trim chicken and marinate two hours. Next, peel, trim and puree mangoes, adding enough juice to make it thin enough to coat lettuce leaves; set dressing aside. In a heavy saute pan, take 1 ounce of oil and toast sesame seeds; set aside. Rub peppers with oil and grill until charred; put in airtight container for 20 minutes. Peel skin from pepper by holding underwater; chop. Rub fennel with oil and grill until soft; chop. Grill and chop pineapple rings. Mix together chopped red bell peppers, pineapple and fennel; chill. Grill chicken. Cool and chop into 1- to 2-inch pieces or cut into 1-inch strips. This can be added to salad warm or chilled. Toss greens with chopped vegetables, fruit, nuts and dressing (pureed mangoes and juice) and sprinkle with chopped chicken and garnish with toasted sesame seeds. Serves four as a main course, or eight as salad served with a meal.

Note: Rodriguez recommends using H.S.M (Herbs, Spices and More) jerk seasoning from Arena, Wis. If interested, call "Bob" at (608) 753-2245.

University Club Tomato Orange and Tarragon Soup

This grand old red brick building on campus and the State Street Mall is like a grandfather watching over the activities of his young. Since 1907, when construction began, the ivy covered exterior has lent a stateliness to decades of eduation mixed with turmoil. Step through the heavy front doors and you become embraced in history. In the backyard is a stone terrace where meals are enjoyed during summer months. Membership is available to the club by contacting manager Juli Johnson.

1 chopped onion
4 chopped garlic cloves
2 Tablespoons olive oil
3 cups V-8
3 cups tomatoes,
skinned and chopped (either canned or fresh)
3 cups orange juice
1 Tablespoon salt
1 Tablespoon pepper
Fresh or dried tarragon, to taste
Saute onion and garlic in olive oil. Add V-8
vegetable juice, tomatoes and orange juice. Then add salt, pepper and tarragon. Simmer and serve or chill.

Sunporch Cafe's Onion Dill Bread

Flavorful and moist, and served with a slice of cheese, it was a "perfect" lunch enjoyed often by Susan Sweeney. Within 12 hours of requesting the recipe from owner Linda Derrickson and her manager, Barb Phelan, I knew that I had a great beginning for my Cooks' Exchange column.

2 extra large eggs
3/4 cup warm buttermilk
3/4 cup warm water
1/4 cup honey
1 Tablespoon molasses
3/4 Tablespoon yeast
1/2 pureed onion
1/4 cup oil
1/2 Tablespoon salt
3 Tablespoons dill weed
2 cups whole wheat flour
4 cups bread flour

In a small bowl, combine extra large eggs, warm buttermilk, warm water, honey, molasses and active dry yeast. Stir well. Skin a yellow onion (approximately 2 inches in diameter) and put half of it in a blender with the oil. While the blender is liquefying the onion, combine salt, dill, whole-wheat flour and the bread flour in a large mixing bowl. Add both liquid mixtures to the flour mixture and knead until all the flour is absorbed. Cover the bowl containing the dough and allow the dough to rest in a warm place until it has doubled in size. Divide and shape the dough, place it in a pan, cover it, and allow it to rise in a warm place until it has doubled in size again. Bake at 350 degrees until the crust is a deep reddish brown.

Note: As it is difficult to mix the dough by hand, kneading by machine is recommended. This is enough dough to make 4 loaves of bread, which bake for 25 to 30 minutes. If small rolls are made, the baking time is 10 to 15 minutes. For a shiny crust, brush the top of the dough with a mixture of egg and water just before placing the dough in the oven.

Artichokes and Tomatoes— From Rossario's Italian Restaurant

The outside flag of verde, bianco e russo (green, white and red) welcomes one to yet another fragment of the old Greenbush neighborhood where Ross Parisi's grandparents and parents settled back in the first quarter of the century. Complemented tastefully with antiques, the interior has a wall of photographs of Italian celebrities and Greenbush "goombahs" (friends). Initially established as a great place for Friday night fish, Rossario's has added Sicilian specialties to share the spotlight with other items from land and sea. Son, Ross, Jr., has already established himself in the business as well as a recent venture in bottling the rich spaghetti sauce customers rate as "the best."

1 small onion, chopped
1/4 cup coarsely chopped walnuts
2 Tablespoons olive oil
3 Tablespoons grated Parmesan cheese
1/2 teaspoon salt
1/8 teaspoon pepper
1/2 cup dry white wine
1/2 cup clam stock or chicken stock
1 Tablespoon fresh basil
1 Tablespoon fresh parsley
1 pint cherry tomatoes, or one 15-ounce can of Italian-style tomatoes, chopped and undrained
One 14-ounce can of artichoke hearts, drained and cut into halves
Tomato paste, optional

Using a 19-inch skillet, saute onions in oil and remove. To same pan, add walnuts, cheese, salt and pepper and stir over medium heat until nuts are coated and golden brown, about 3 to 4 minutes. Add wine, clam stock, parsley and basil and simmer 3 to 4 minutes. Return onions to skillet and add tomatoes and cook about 3 to 4

minutes. Add artichokes and continue cooking for an
additional 3 to 4 minutes. This should be a consistency to
toss with heavier type pastas such as penne or fusilli. If
you prefer a thicker sauce, a tiny amount of tomato paste
can be added.

Yield: 4 servings

CHICKEN SCALOPPINE PICCATA–
ANTONIO'S ITALIAN RESTARAUNT

Tony Schiavo and his family serve generations of mouthwatering Sicilian masterpieces at 1109 S. Park Street. With the melodic background of Luciano Pavarotti, Schiavo, his wife, Rosemary; his mother, Marian Amato Schiavo; and his sons, Nick and Jim, offer a special fragment of the old Greenbush neighborhood. For it was there that food such as this was prepared for more than half a century by the families who brought their cooking skills from their native villages in Sicily. Two were the Amato's and the Schiavo's. Madison is lucky to have Antonio's and all the love that goes into everything they prepare.

Two 6-ounce boneless skinless chicken breasts
Flour
Salt and pepper
1 garlic clove, minced
2 Tablespoons olive oil
4 ounces dry white wine
4 ounces low-salt chicken broth
Wedge of fresh lemon
1 Tablespoon capers, drained

Lightly pound chicken breasts between two sheets of waxed paper. Dip in flour seasoned with salt and pepper and shake off excess flour. Heat oil and saute chicken until lightly browned. Remove to heated plate. Add garlic to pan and saute 1 minute. Add wine, chicken broth and juice from lemon wedge and cook on medium-high flame to reduce liquid to about one-third, or until a glazelike consistency to coat a spoon. Return chicken to pan with capers and heat through.

Seven Pines Inn
Lewis, Polk County, Wis.

Off the beaten path

. . . . •

THERE ARE TREASURES TO BE FOUND IN THE WOODS OF WISCONSIN. WHILE SEARCHING FOR A SPECIAL PLACE TO CELEBRATE OUR 33RD WEDDING ANNIVERSARY, MY HUSBAND AND I DISCOVERED A GEM IN THE NORTHWEST Indianhead section of the state in upper Polk County. Around one of the few corners in Lewis was a country road a long stone's throw from Highway 35 that took us past fields, up and down a few hills and to a turn into the woods on a path so narrow that branches brushed our car as we made our way, finally, to a small clearing that is home to Seven Pines Lodge. Teddy Roosevelt would have loved Sevens Pines Lodge. And he would have respected the self- made millionaire Charles Lewis, who sensed future destruction of the virgin white pine forest and bought 680 acres to protect them from loggers. In 1903, Lewis hired a Norwegian woodworker and two assistants to build a lodge in the depths of the forest alongside a rushing stream. The lodge was named Seven Pines after the seven largest pines that stood guard over it. Secluded and still amazingly pristine today, the lodge and its cabins provide a storybook setting for visitors wishing to stay overnight or to stop in and dine at the restaurant that offers rustic dining inside or on the wrap around porch that overlooks Knapp Creek. The creek is a private trout stream protected by the Department of Natural Resources. Claiming 5,500 trout per square mile, the stream is yet another jewel for those who belong to the lodge's fly fishing club. When a visitor chooses trout for dinner, the fish is taken fresh from the stream, along with watercress from its banks for garnish. Among the many truly welcoming complements to this magical woodsy scene, Seven Pines remains as it was when President Calvin Coolidge stayed there. Original furnishings

- decorate its rooms and the snowshoes and skis its builders wore while trudging through the snow to work hang above the massive stone living room fireplace. Recent complements include impressive woodcarvings purchased in Germany by owner Lee Gohlike. Because meals at the inn are fixed price, reservations are necessary. Having spent the past 50 summers on a lake 20-some miles away and never hearing before this year of the Seven Pines, it merely reinforces the many treasures that lie waiting in the woods of Wisconsin.

Ann's French Tomato and Avocado with Leaf Lettuce– The Seven Pines Lodge, Lewis, Wisconsin

Truly off the beaten track, the inn is hidden from the rest of the world by a heavy dose of Mother Nature. Built in 1903 to protect the area from loggers, the inn is a return to the past in a story book setting that includes watercress growing in abundance alongside a rushing stream with 5,500 trout per mile, many of which are served immediately after being caught. Chef Ann Ward inaugurates many a meal with a peeled tomato deliciously seasoned and stuffed with avocado.

Lower tomatoes in boiling water for 10 seconds or more until skins slip off easily. Peel and scoop out insides of tomatoes, being careful not to puncture bottoms. Turn shells upside down until ready to use. Prepare French Dressing, using recipe below, and assemble tomatoes as directed.

FRENCH DRESSING:
2 Tablespoons tomato ketchup
2 Tablespoons red wine vinegar
1/2 Tablespoon Worcestershire sauce
1 teaspoon salt
Pinch dry mustard
Small garlic clove, minced
Pepper
10 Tablespoons olive oil
Avocados, peeled
Tomatoes, peeled
Crumbled bacon
Chopped chives; Fresh basil, minced; Watercress to garnish, optional Combine ketchup, vinegar, Worcestershire, salt, mustard, garlic and pepper. Slowly add olive oil. Peel avocados and dice into small chunks, along with additional peeled tomatoes. Marinate in some of the French dressing. To assemble, place peeled,

• drained, empty whole tomatoes on leaf lettuce. Just before serving, salt and pepper cavity of each tomato and fill with marinated avocados and tomatoes. Spoon an additional 1/2 tablespoon (or more) of French dressing over each filling. Sprinkle with crumbled bacon, chopped chives and fresh chopped basil. Garnish with a sprig of watercress.

Bird's Nest Basket—
The Sandhill Inn, Merrimac

In a century-old Victorian home on Highway 78 in Merrimac, Chef Paul Short, Sara Bancroft-Short and Gen Bancroft offer an unforgetable Sandhill experience with hand-picked items and wildlife from the many hiding places of Wisconsin.

2 Idaho potatoes, 100 ct. size
Oil for frying (enough to fill fryer)
Wire basket liners

Heat oil to 375 degrees and leave baskets in oil to season them while oil is heating. Peel and shred the potatoes. Soak them in warm water. Drain the warm water and soak them with warm water again. Remove the warm water and pat the potatoes dry. Carefully line wire baskets with shredded potatoes. Close the baskets and fry until potato baskets are golden brown. Carefully tap out baskets and cool on paper towels to remove excess oil.

Note: Prepare extra potato baskets for those that might break upon release. Baskets are available at kitchen specialty shops or by mail order from Williams-Sonoma.

Boder's Blueberry or Cherry Muffins

Established as a tea room in 1929, Boder's-on-the-River in Mequon, Wis. is a study of the type of harvest a family can expect year after year with hard work, respect, togetherness, and great chefs. Boder's is such a place. The restaurant is known for homemade meals, but their muffins also rate at the top of the list of favorites, especially when the batter has been speckled with hand picked Wisconsin fruit.

2 cups sifted flour
4 teaspoons baking powder
3/4 cup sugar
1 teaspoon salt
1 cup frozen or canned blueberries (drained) or 1 cup frozen or canned tart cherries (drained)
2 eggs
1/2 cup melted butter
1 cup milk
CINNAMON AND SUGAR TOPPING:
1/8 teaspoon cinnamon
1/2 cup sugar

Place paper cups in ungreased muffin tins. Sift dry ingredients together in large bowl.

Add blueberries or cherries to dry mix and mix until well coated. In a small bowl, beat eggs well. Add melted butter and milk. Quickly stir liquid mixture into dry mix. Do not overmix as overblending will cause a tough texture. Fill muffin cups full and sprinkle lightly with cinnamon topping. Bake at 400 degrees for 20 minutes or until brown.

Makes 12-14 muffins.

Baked Brie with Cognac Pecan Sauce– The Red Circle Inn, Nashotah, WI

An elegant touch to a slice of soft mellow cheese, served at an inn with the history of an 1847 hotel-tavern-dining room-stagecoach stop. The inn has tasted the good life with territorial development, a romantic era of summer residents, a disruptive fire, and many other hurdles in its years. Yet, with its Old World charm and outstanding meals, the inn's reputation carries on in Nashotah.

1 cup cognac (can substitute brandy if necessary)
1/2 cup brown sugar
1/2 cup pecans
1/2 pound butter
1 pound brie cheese

Over low heat melt the butter and slowly add pecans, cook for 2 minutes. Slowly add brown sugar and cook until sugar has turned into syrup. Add cognac and cook out alcohol (when flame is no longer present). Pour mixture over slightly melted brie and serve with crackers and/or fruit slices.

Black Bean Chili with Sirloin and Creme Fraiche— Clay Market Cafe, Cambridge, WI

Cambridge is a treasure chest filled with jewels. A little east of Madison, this town is ever anxious to please. Surprises abound and one just happens to be the Clay Market Cafe.

1 pound dry black beans
1 Tablespoon ground cumin
1/2 teaspoon cayenne
2 teaspoons paprika
1 Tablespoon dried oregano
3 Tablespoons chili powder
1 bay leaf
1 Tablespoon oil
1 yellow onion, peeled and chopped
4 garlic cloves, peeled and minced
Green bell pepper, seeded and finely chopped
4 large tomatoes, cored and roughly chopped
1 jalapeno pepper, seeded
1/2 cup cilantro leaves
1 pound grilled sirloin steak, cut into half-inch cubes
Salt and Pepper to taste

Pour the beans into a colander and rinse under running water, sorting through them for stones. Bring beans to a boil in water to cover by 4 inches. Boil approximately 1 hour. The beans will soak up water, so you may need to add more water while boiling. Beans will be tender but not broken when done. Heat a dry skillet over medium heat and toast the cumin, cayenne, paprika, oregano, chili powder and bay leaf until they start to become fragrant. (Be careful not to let them burn). Heat the oil in a saucepan and saute the onion, garlic and green pepper over medium heat until soft and translucent, about 5 minutes. Add the toasted spices, tomatoes and a sprinkling of salt and pepper and saute for 15 minutes, stirring occasionally. Add the vegetable mixture to the beans, along with water to cover by 2 inches. Simmer, covered, for 20 minutes. Saute sirloin cubes over high heat until medium rare. Cut into fine pieces. Adjust seasoning in the beans and add the chopped cilantro, jalapeno and sirloin. Simmer for another 10 minutes. Serve in bowls with a dollop of creme fraiche (optional).

CREME FRAICHE:

1/2 cup buttermilk

4 cups heavy cream

Combine and leave out for approximately 8 hours. Refrigerate and serve when chilled.

ROUND BARN HOUSE DRESSING— SPRING GREEN, WI

As you break away from the Great River Road, pick up Highway 14 south of LaCrosse, and enter Spring Green, you will notice to your left a large round barn. Stop by to spend the evening, or at least long enough for a memorable and relaxing meal in the shadows of a Frank Lloyd Wright addition. With that touch of fame, here is another . . . their famous house dressing.

6 cups vinegar
5 cups sugar
2 cups oil
1 teaspoon garlic salt
1 small onion, minced fine
2 cups water
Mix well by hand.
Makes 1 gallon.

Dairy Fresh White Cheddar Melts— The Machine Shed, Rockford, IL

It takes a little more than an hour to drive from Madison to the "heart of America" in Rockford to sample Mike Whalen's dream. His Iowa based company started as a seed planted with the love of state raised hogs and succulent pork dishes prepared with pride by his family. This "praise the pig and pass the mashed potato" place sparkles with the smiles, generosity and good flavor of rural America.

1 pound Wisconsin white Cheddar cheese curds
2 cups dry batter mix
1 cup water or beer
1/2 cup flour

Place cheese curds in a nonstick, greased cake pan. Bake at 200 degrees until curds are melted flat in the pan. Place in cooler for 1 hour. Cut into 2-inch squares. Prepare batter mix by combining with water or beer. Dredge cheese squares in flour, then thoroughly coat them with batter mix. Deep-fry until golden brown. Remove and place on paper towel to absorb grease. Serve with barbecue dipping sauce.

Hoffman House–
Kentucky Pie (Ishnala, WI)

Yet another Wisconsin gem, Ishnala, hidden among the woods and nestled at the edge of a cliff, retains its magic, year after year, with the solitude of the past. This is truly a slice of nostalgia for countless thousands of residents and visitors alike.

2 cups all-purpose flour
1 teaspooon salt
2/3 cup shotening
5-7 Tablespoons cold water

In a large bowl combine flour and salt. Using an electric mixer, cut in shortening until particles are size of small peas. Sprinkle mixture with water, 1 Tablespoon at a time, while tossing and mixing lightly with a fork. Add water until dough is just moist enough to hold together. Form dough into a ball. Place on well-floured surface. Flatten ball slightly. Sprinkle top of dough lightly with flour. Also, coat rolling pin with flour to prevent sticking. Roll dough to a circle one inch larger than a 10-inch pie tin. Place dough in pan. Fold edge of pastry under, even with rim, and trim excess crust. Crust is now ready for filling.

FILLING:
3 eggs
3/4 cup brown sugar
3/4 cup sugar
1 2/3 cups flour
1 teaspoon vanilla
12 ounces chopped pecans
1 1/2 cups melted butter
2 ounces heavy cream
9 ounces semi sweet mini chocolate chips

Preheat oven to 325 degrees. In large bowl, beat eggs until foamy. Beat in flour, both sugars, vanilla and heavy cream until well-blended. Blend in melted butter. Stir in chocolate chips and pecans. Pour into pie shell. Bake at 325 degrees for one hour and 15 minutes.

TOPPING:

2/3 cup sugar

3 1/3 Tablespoons butter

5 1/3 Tablespoons milk

2/3 cup chocolate chips

1/2 cup chopped pecans

Place sugar, butter and milk in saucepan. Bring to a boil, stir constantly for one minute. Add chocolate chips, simmer and stir for an additional minute. Using a teaspoon, drizzle topping over pie. Sprinkle with pecans. Refrigerate pie.

SERVING THE PIE:

Cut pie into serving portions and heat individual pieces in microwave oven 45-60 seconds. Serve with vanilla ice cream.

Mr. G's Corn Fritters with Honey Butter– Mr G's Arlington, WI

Although the recipe makes a large amount of fritters, former owner Claudine Alford was happy to share what brings in droves of diners on Tuesdays to enjoy with homemade chicken and dumplings, and on Wednesdays with "sweeter-than-cod" whitefish or barbecued ribs.

10 eggs, separated
Two (16-ounce) cans whole kernel corn, drained well, saving juices
Two (16-ounce) cans cream-style corn
3/4 cup reserved corn juice, adding milk if necessary
3/4 cup milk
1 teaspoon salt
4 Tablespoons baking powder
8 to 8 1/2 cups all-purpose flour

Separate eggs and beat egg whites until stiff and dry. In another bowl, beat egg yolks lightly until mixed, but do not whip. Add both types of corn, juice and milk. Mix together dry ingredients and add to corn mixture. Fold in stiffly beaten egg whites. Refrigerate until ready to use. Using a small ice cream scoop, drop batter into deep fryer. These should look like hush puppies; however, just because they become a golden crispy brown doesn't mean they are done inside. Insert a knife in a fried fritter until it comes out dry, just as when testing pumpkin or custard pies.

HONEY BUTTER:
3 pounds butter
1 1/2 pounds honey
1 pound powdered sugar
Cinnamon, optional

Whip butter, then add remaining ingredients, mix well.

Twice Baked Potatoes– The Sandhill Inn, Merrimac, WI

Thanks to Betty Wipperfurth, Middleton, a door was opened to the Sandhill Inn for readers unaware of its many treasures.

4 Birds Nest Baskets (see recipe, page 167)
4 potatoes, 100 ct. size
2 green onions, finely chopped
1/2 cup Parmesan cheese
1/4 cup whole milk
1/8 cup sour cream
Salt and white pepper, to taste

Peel potatoes and cook them until soft. Push the potatoes through a ricer. Whisk in the green onions, Parmesan cheese, whole milk, sour cream and season with salt and white pepper. Place mixture in a pastry bag with a star tip and pipe into a birds nest basket. Place into baking dish and bake at 400 degrees for approximately 15 minutes or until golden brown. Drizzle butter on cooked twice-baked potato and sprinkle with Parmesan cheese.

Scallops of Provimi Veal New Orleans– The Red Circle Inn, Nashotah, WI

When owners Mark and Renee Manion were asked for a beef stroganoff recipe served during the 1970s, I was told that the chef who prepared that particular recipe was no longer employed there. So as not to disappoint me, the Manions shared two other recipes that are very popular with today's guests.

24-ounce trimmed Provimi veal tenderloin

1 red pepper, julienned

1/2 small onion, julienned

1 diced tomato

1 cup white wine

8 fresh shrimp, 16/20-count, peeled and deveined

1 ounce chopped garlic

1 cup Paul Prudhomme's Cajun seasonings

8 ounces butter, melted

1 cup flour

1 cup dry white wine

Cut tenderloin into 2-ounce medallions. Pound until 1/4-inch thick with a meat mallot. Mix flour with 1 cup Cajun seasonings. Dredge veal scallops in the flour. Direction for preparing one portion: Heat sautee pan on medium heat. Add 1 ounce butter and warm. Add 2 shrimp and cook for 2 minutes. Add one-fourth of the onions, peppers and tomatoes and cook 2 minutes. Remove from the pan and reheat the pan on high. Add 1 ounce butter and saute 6 ounces of the veal 1 minute per side. Return shrimp and vegetables to pan to reheat. Add 2 ounces white wine and cook until wine is reduced by half.

Recipe can serve 4.

Serving suggestion: Angel hair pasta or rice pilaf make excellent accompaniments.

Severson's Gas Station
Reierson photo courtesy of Joe Hermolin

Monty Schiro, Monty's Blue Plate Diner
Photo by Joel Heiman

The new old East Side

. . . . •

IF "STOMPING GROUND" MEANS A WALKING
DISTANCE FROM HOME THAT OFFERS JUST ABOUT
EVERY CONVENIENCE TO FUEL A SMALL TOWN PLUS
PROVIDES A PLACE WHERE FRIENDS CAN MEET,
THEN ATWOOD AVENUE WAS MY STOMPING
GROUND. Between Lowell School and Schenk's Corner on
Madison's East Side was a strip of blue-collar, working-class
hominess. Available were all the amenities of a flourishing business
district - bakeries, restaurants, drugstores, barbershops, beauty
parlors, clothing stores, two bowling alleys, two music stores,
churches and a small, family-owned grocery store on almost every
block. There was a photographer, a florist, a jeweler, a tailor and a
tiny millinery shop with hats of every shape and color.

Our Ben Franklin store had two entrances and long aisles to
accommodate baby turtles and goldfish, trading cards, yarn, cobalt
bottles of Evening in Paris cologne, plus thousands of other
necessities. The East Side Business Men's Association clubhouse
across the street from St. Bernard Catholic School made a strong
civic statement, with a factory a block away in one direction, a
lumber company in the other and a fuel company forming a
triangle at the railroad tracks on Corry Street behind the church.
Sporting goods, hardware and furniture stores speckled the area
with the usual abundance of small taverns to serve as gathering
spots during evening hours. A root beer stand occupied one corner
and a red brick fire station sat on another a mere hop, skip and
jump from the Dutch Maid Ice Cream Shop, with its long counter
and short stools, while Dixie Cream Donut Shop nearby had a
short counter with long rows of doughnuts.

Transactions took place behind the pillars of the imposing

Security State Bank, and on the other side of the street at an angle was the Schenk-Huegel General Store, with a machine that showed the bones of your feet through shoes to determine a proper fit. On the second floors of many buildings were the offices of doctors, dentists and lawyers.

Entertainment was provided by the Eastwood Theatre, where stars twinkled in the black "skies" overhead, even during afternoon matinees. And with the help of Ethyl and the many gas stations that zig-zagged the avenue, the area remained mobile. Except for a hospital, it seemed we had everything we needed. It was a wonderful neighborhood, nurturing me as a parent would with good, wholesome examples to follow while I hung out with friends. One day the music stopped and the vibrant strip of humanity all but died. Years of patience followed, with optimism that filled vacant buildings but only for short periods. It wasn't until recently that, finally, newly planted seeds took hold and Atwood Avenue began to blossom once again. A part of the recent renaissance is Monty's Blue Plate Diner, located at 2089 Atwood Ave. in a gas station once owned by Ole Severson, later by the Havey brothers, and today by Monty Schiro. In 1990, the building lost its last evidence of gas tanks and oil pans, replaced with the sleek design of architect Ed Linville. The contemporary diner is decorated with pictures of the 1930s and 1940s, when the country loved mashed potatoes and meatloaf. You will find both dishes on the menu at Monty's with other old favorites, new favorites, many vegetarian items and the desserts you might remember tasting at grandma's house. Behind the swinging kitchen doors is a tall, red-haired cook with a smile that lingers despite the heat and bustle in the room in which he operates. Tim Lloyd delights customers daily with everything he prepares, especially the homemade soups he boasts as his specialty. These kettles of innovation are ladled alongside orders that bring back a bit of yesterday and the Atwood Avenue I remember along with new ideas for another generation to recall someday.

Monty's Blue Plate Diner-Reuben Soup

3 Tablespoons vegetable oil
1 large onion, diced fine
6 stalks celery, diced fine, including leaves
2 pounds sauerkraut, canned or bagged (found in refrigerated section)
1 pound corned beef, diced fine
4 quarts water
1 cup butter
1 cup flour
1 pound Swiss cheese, diced fine or shredded
Salt; Pepper; Tabasco sauce; Caraway seed (adds a nice touch)
2 cups cream, heavy or half and half
2 cubes chicken bouillon

In large saucepan or kettle, saute onion and celery in vegetable oil. Add sauerkraut, simmering while stirring for about 10 minutes. Add corned beef, simmer and stir for 10 minutes. Add water and bring to slow boil. Let boil for 30 minutes.

Thicken with roux made with butter and flour by melting butter in saucepan and gradually adding flour. Cook until mixture forms a thick brown paste. Add this to soup, 1 tablespoon at a time, whisking vigorously to smooth out any lumps. A little less than 2 cups will thicken this soup. Add Swiss cheese. Season to taste with salt, pepper, Tabasco sauce, caraway seed, cream and chicken boullion. Cook another 10-15 minutes to blend flavors.

Serves 10 to 12.

JOLLY BOB'S JERK JOINT
SWEET POTATO SALAD

Another old neighborhood experiencing new life is Williamson Street. Referred to by many as "Willy Street, "it has become home to a variety of people and flavors, such as Tim Erickson and his sky-blue "jerk joint." Leave Madison at the curb to walk through the door that leads you to a warm remote island with Caribbean-style cuisine. The music tells you so. And so will the food. Deep fried sweet potatoes, curry chicken wings in peanut sauce, jerk chicken, pork and fish served on banana leaves. Some hot. Some not. Casual attire, just like an island eatery. And that's just a sample of why you'll want to return.

4 medium sweet potatoes, peeled and cut into 3/4-inch pieces
1/2 each red, yellow and green bell peppers, seeded and cut into 1/4-inch pieces
1/2 large red onion, diced small
4 to 6 Tablespoons finely chopped fresh parsley

DRESSING:
3 Tablespoons Dijon mustard
3 Tablespoons ketchup
1 Tablespoon minced garlic
3/4 cup olive oil
4 Tablespoons cider vinegar
1 Tablespoon Worcestershire sauce
Juice of one large lime
Salt to taste and plenty of freshly cracked black pepper

Boil sweet potato cubes in salted water for 10 to 12 minutes. Cook until fork tender but firm. Don't overcook or salad will be mushy. When potatoes are done, drain and immediately pour cold water over them to stop the cooking. Keep pouring cold water until potatoes stop steaming and are cool to the touch throughout. Mix cooled potatoes with diced peppers, onion and parsley. Make dressing by placing mustard, ketchup and garlic in medium-sized bowl.

Whisking constantly, add olive oil in slow steady stream. After blending well, add vinegar, Worcestershire sauce, lime juice, salt and pepper and mix well. Pour dressing over potato mixture and toss gently. Serve immediately or keep covered in refrigerator for up to five days.

CHOCOLATE CHUNK CHEESECAKE–MADISON BAGEL CO.

Back in the early 1960s I visited an appliance center on Atwood Avenue to purchase a radio-phonograph console for the apartment I was renting in the century-old Simeon Mills mansion at 2709 Sommers Avenue. For years the avenue had been like a small town supplying area residents with almost everything of importance. Things changed, however, when outlying shopping malls drew people away from the neighborhood to where an abundance of variety was at their fingertips and the elements never dampened their shopping spirits. Overnight it seemed that the many blocks of daylight stores and evening lights on Atwood Avenue became nothing more than nostalgia. We remembered the good days and wondered if things would ever be the same again. Although things seldom return to their original state, Atwood Avenue, is once again alive and well. The windows of the former appliance center now sport tables and chairs for diners to enjoy breakfast, lunch and dinner, cream cheese on freshly made bagels, and delicious desserts like chocolate chunk cheesecake.

FILLING:

2 1/2 pounds Neufachtel cream cheese

1 1/2 cups sugar

4 eggs

1 Tablespoon vanilla

CRUST:

Oreo cookies, (about 1 cup crumbs)

CHUNKS:

1 pound bittersweet or semisweet chocolate;

2/3 cup butter

1/3 cup strongly brewed coffee

4 eggs

1 1/2 cups sugar

1/2 cup flour

1/2 pound walnuts

Chocolate chuncks: Prepare ahead of time (a few hours

or the night before). Melt together chocolate, butter and coffee. Set aside. Beat eggs on high until frothy (about two minutes). Add sugar slowly, beating after each addition. Add chocolate mixture. Add flour and walnuts. Do not overmix. Pour into a 9-by-13-inch pan and bake at 350 degrees for approximately 20 minutes, or until edges are set. Cool and refrigerate. (The chocolate needs to be firm.) When ready to use, cut into 1-inch cubes.

Note: you will be using only about half the pan of chocolate for the cheesecake. Cheesecake filling: Cream together Neufchatel and sugar until smooth. Add eggs one at a time, mixing each one into mixture. Add vanilla. Set aside. Crust: Crumble Oreos to make 1 cup of crumbs. Press cookie crumbs into a sprayed 9-inch springform pan. Layer cream cheese filling and the chocolate chunks cut into 1-inch cubes. Bake at 300 degrees for about two hours or until center is set. Cool. Refrigerate until ready to serve. Makes 12-16 servings.

KEY LIME RUM CHEESECAKE, MRS. MILLER'S BAKERY

On an unpretentious corner in an unpretentious building, the Williamson Street Co-op serves people from all over Madison. If you happen to live in the neighborhood, consider yourself lucky to be within walking distance. What began back in 1973 as a full-service neighborhood grocery store specializing in natural and organically-grown foods today is stronger than ever giving us reason to applaud those who have made it work so well. If you haven't been there before, visit and study what they offer. In the deli was a dessert that Betty G. wanted to make at home. We needed permission from the baker at Mrs. Miller's Bakery, as well as the Willy Street Co-op owners. Both were happy to share.

CRUST:
1/2 cup flour
1/4 cup powdered sugar
4 Tablespoons butter, cold, unsalted

FILLING:
2 pounds (32 ounces) cream cheese, softened
1 1/3 cups sugar
1 Tablespoon cornstarch
6 extra-large eggs
1/2 cup Nellie & Joe's Key Lime Juice (see note)
3/8 cup rum (Bacardi Light)

TOPPING:
1/3 cup graham cracker crumbs
1 1/2 teaspoons sugar
1/8 teaspoon cinnamon
1 Tablespoon unsalted butter, melted

CRUST:
Cut butter into small pieces, put into food processor with flour and powdered sugar. Process briefly until butter is cut into very small pieces but not completely blended with flour. Spread evenly across bottom of 9-inch cake pan (do not pat down). Bake at 350 degrees for 15 to 20 minutes until light brown.

FILLING:

Mix cream cheese, sugar and cornstarch together until smooth. Scrape bowl, add eggs one at a time, scrape bowl again. Add juice, then rum. If mixture separates (looks grainy), then blend in food processor until smooth.

Pour batter into pan. Topping: Mix graham cracker crumbs, sugar and cinnamon together. Stir in melted butter. Sprinkle entire top of cheesecake with mixture. Bake at 225 degrees for 1 hour or 1 hour 15 minutes, until cake looks "set" when shaken gently and cake rises about 1/2 inch. Cool on wire rack. If cake cracks, fill in crack by pushing graham cracker crumbs into it.

Chill cheesecake in pan. To remove, run thin knife or spatula along sides. Place pan over very low heat on stove burner for a few seconds to heat bottom. Place plate or cardboard circle over cheesecake. Turn over quickly but carefully. Lift pan up an inch. Shake pan or rap on plate so that cake falls out. Then using another plate or circle, flip right side up.

Serves 16.

Note: Nellie & Joe's Key Lime Juice is bottled with juice extracted from Key limes in Key West and can be purchased at some stores in Madison. It is excellent for Key Lime Pie. Remember to refrigerate after opening.

SESAME NOODLE SALAD—HARMONY BAR AND GRILL

From 1944 to 1980, the Karabis family owned and operated this corner bar at the corner of Atwood Avenue and Dunning Street. Adding to the friendliness of the establishment was a parrot that greeted each customer who came in for a cold beer, homemade meals and the succulent Greek flavor of the family's famous Spartan sandwich. Today, Keith Daniels and Mary Jo Ragozzino are in command as husband and wife. Expansion of the interior without losing the charm of the old neighborhood bar remains on their list of priorities as well as adding tasty charm to the reliable bar food with the addition of new food items. Ragozzino, a product of a Brooklyn, NY Italian family, once baked a birthday cake for Frank Sinatra. It's no surprise that with her creative touches in the kitchen she has added her family's recipe for homemade pizza to the menu.

1/2 pound linguine
1 Tablespoon 100 percent pure sesame oil
3 medium carrots, thinly sliced
1 cup red cabbage, finely chopped
1/2 cup black olives, drained and sliced
6 to 9 green onions, thinly sliced
3 Tablespoons lightly toasted sesame seeds
DRESSING:
1/4 cup soy sauce
2 Tablespoons sesame oil
1 1/2 teaspoons hot chili oil

Cook pasta until al dente. Drain and toss with 1 tablespoon sesame oil. Add carrots, cabbage, olives and green onions to cooled pasta.

Whisk together dressing, add to above with the cooled sesame seeds, and refrigerate. Toss before serving. Serve at room temperature.

Yield: 4 to 5 servings.

Mariano Sansone, Natale Troia, Mr. Badena, Settimo Intravaia, Cologero Intravaia, and a writer who moved from the neighborhood and out of town. Gathered together to quench their thirst on a hot summer day in the backyard of the old Troia store on the corner of Desmond (Bowen) Court and Murray Street – about 1920. Notice opened cans of caponatina (eggplant relish).

Mangia! Mangia! Eat! Eat!

. . . . •

ITALIANS LOVE TO CELEBRATE. GIVE THEM A REASON AND WITHIN HOURS THE KITCHEN HUMS WITH ACTIVITY AS THE HOUSE EXUDES MOUTH WATERING AROMAS. Memorable feasts can be simple, but above all, don't forget the pasta, al dente. There are few "correct" ways to cook pasta, yet each Italian household in every Little Italy of America seems to have its own method. One was described to me by the daughter of Sicilian immigrants who settled in the Greenbush neighborhood about 85 years ago.

She referred to the procedure as a "litany"–repetition of something brought by her mother from the village she left behind and which probably was taught by her grandmother. This is what family tradition is all about.

...

While the unfamiliar aromas were carried by lake breezes from the corners of Park and Regent Streets, Italian and Sicilian men were busy planting seeds and roots for grapevines, fruit trees, flowers, vegetables, and grass. And, as the low swampy grounds that skirted Lake Monona blossomed into an ethnic village, tiny family restaurants began serving food never imagined by longtime Madison residents. Eventually word spread, drawing people to the neighborhood they had previously avoided. Little did skeptics realize, many decades later Madisonians would bathe in the glory of garlic, pasta and tomato sauce as the most popular food in America.

...

I like to refer to the old Greenbush neighborhood as a treasure chest of culture. Around each corner, down every street, lingering in every alley was the sweet aroma of pane (bread), arancini (rice balls), caponatina (eggplant relish), salsiccia (sausage) and the mouth watering staple of thick red pomodori (tomato) sauce that simmered for hours in large kettles on back burners for evening meals. The triangular shaped settlement was a diamond in the rough, for it seemed that only those who lived within its confines were aware of their precious surroundings. Everything disappeared in the 1960s when urban renewal made its mark throughout America and claimed the Madison property bordered by Park and Regent streets and West Washington Avenue, leaving behind only the roots of grapevines and poignant memories.

SICILIAN OLIVE SALAD

Anne Sorrentino writes a monthly food column for Fra Noi, the Italian newspaper of Chicagoland. She is a friend, a fine cook and food authority, having edited several Italian cookbooks. When John Caliva, Madison, wanted to make olive salad like his grandmother Caruso made years ago in her kitchen on Mound Street in the old Greenbush neighborhood, I remembered and referred to Sorrentino's favorite recipe.

1 pound Italian green olives
1 large onion, chopped
1 large clove garlic, halved
1/2 cup sliced celery
Crushed red pepper to taste
1/4 cup wine vinegar
1 Tablespoon fresh basil, chopped, or 1 teaspoon dry basil
1/2 teaspoon oregano
1/2 cup olive oil
Salt and pepper

Wash olives and dry on paper towels. Crack each olive with a mallet or bottom of a heavy cup. Leave stones intact. Combine olives with remaining ingredients and mix well. Keep refrigerated in a covered jar at least two days. Use as a side dish or part of an antipasto tray. Excellent as a snack with Italian bread.

Note: This will keep for an indefinite period.

Uncooked Fresh Tomato Sauce

Not all spaghetti sauce should simmer for hours on the back burner. In fact, it is said that two hours is the maximum time necessary for peak flavor. A reader of my column in the Wisconsin State Journal wanted something even quicker to serve over pasta. It doesn't get any easier, or fresher, than this.

1 pound red ripe plum tomatoes
1 garlic clove
1 shallot clove
4 fresh basil leaves
Salt and pepper, to taste
1/4 teaspoon dried red pepper flakes
1/2 cup olive oil

Peel tomatoes and remove hard stem. Cut into small cubes and remove seeds by squeezing with hands. Place in a blender or food processor with the garlic, shallot, basil, salt, black and red peppers and olive oil. Blend at high speed for one or two seconds, or until the tomatoes are somewhat crushed and combined with the other ingredients. Do not overblend. Serve at room temperature.

Makes about 2 cups, or enough sauce for 1/2 pound of spaghetti.

Note: For a sweeter sauce, add a pinch or two of sugar.

Lucy Gervasi Corona's Special Garlic Sauce

As a remnant of the old Greenbush neighborhood and the Gervasi-Corona families who resided at the corners of Regent and Murray Streets, this sauce had enough surprise ingredients to be recognized with an honorable mention in the Wisconsin State Journal 1963 cookbook contest.

1 whole head of garlic, crushed

1/4 cup steak sauce

1/2 cup ketchup

3/4 cup oil

1 Tablespoon oregano

1 teaspoon sweet basil

Juice of one lemon

1 teaspoon salt

1 teaspoon pepper

4 ounces burgundy Tomato juice

Crush garlic in quart jar. Combine remaining ingredients in jar and fill with tomato juice. Keep in refrigerator. Use on steak, chicken or fish.

Note: Sugar can be added if a sweeter sauce is desired.

MUFFALETTA

This is a New Orleans creation that quickly found popularity in other Italian settlements across America. Tracy Swanson described something similar to what she ordered at a tiny restaurant on South Park Street back in the 1950s, but could not remember the name of the restaurant or the sandwich. Steven Keip responded with his recipe for muffaletta with olive salad.

24 ounces Genoa-style salami
24 ounces sugar-cured ham
24 ounces Provolone cheese
Olive salad (recipe below)
8 Kaiser rolls

To assemble sandwich, have the butcher or deli person slice the salami, ham and cheese very thin. Arrange 3 ounces of each of the above on Kaiser rolls. Top with 2 tablespoons of the Olive Salad. Makes 8 sandwiches.

OLIVE SALAD:

1 cup green salad olives, drained and finely chopped
3 Tablespoons olive oil
1 teaspoon dried basil
1 teaspoon dried oregano
1 Tablespoon minced garlic

Drain olives well and chop finely. Add remaining ingredients and stir well. Refrigerate until ready to use.

Pasta E Fagioli
(Pasta with Beans)

Because few franchises can share recipes, I returned home to one of the books I wrote for an authentic pasta e fagioli from an old Sicilian Greenbush family. In Volume II of, "A Taste of Memories from the Old 'Bush,'" there was one submitted by Rose Troia McCormick in memory of her mother, Lena Troia. A variation made by Rose's sister, Jacki Troia White, appears at the bottom of the page. Lena taught her daughters well.

1 1/4 cups dried kidney beans
1 large onion, diced
2-3 garlic cloves, minced
6-7 ripe tomatoes, peeled and diced
2 small stalks of celery, diced
1/2 cup olive oil
3 Tablespoons tomato puree
1 bay leaf
1/2 teaspoon dried basil
1 teaspoon dried oregano
1 Tablespoon parsley
Salt and pepper to taste
10 to 12 cups water
1 cup ditalini or broken spaghetti, uncooked;
Grated Parmesan cheese

Soak dried beans overnight. The next morning, drain and rinse beans and place in soup kettle with water, onions and garlic; cook for 2 hours until beans are tender. In another large pan, cook tomatoes and celery for about 30 minutes until mushy. Add to soup kettle and simmer for 30 minutes. Add remaining ingredients, except for pasta and cheese, and cook for an additional 30 minutes. Add pasta to boiling mixture and stir well. Turn off heat and allow to sit for 10 to 15 minutes or until pasta is al dente. Sprinkle each bowlful with grated Parmesan and serve. Serves 6 to 8. *Note: For a stronger flavor, add 2 packets of broth seasoning or 2 boullion cubes. Jackie Troia White substitutes a head of escarole for the celery.*

INSALATA DI PENNE CON TONNO E BROCOLLI, (PASTA SALAD WITH TUNA AND BROCOLLI)

A telephone request was received one day for a pasta salad made with tuna fish and black olives. You'll find this on the menu at Ciro and Sal's Restaurant in Provincetown, Mass.

1 bunch fresh broccoli
1 pound white tuna or swordfish
1 pound penne (pasta)
4 ripe tomatoes, cored and cut into thin wedges
1 pound fresh mozzarella, cut into 1/4-inch cubes
8 black olives, cut into thin slivers
1/2 cup walnuts, toasted
4 garlic cloves, finely chopped
2 Tablespoons chopped fresh parsley
Salt and freshly ground black pepper
4 anchovy fillets, rinsed and dried
3/4 cup extra virgin olive oil

Put a large pot of salted water on to boil for the penne. Separate all broccoli flowerets from stalks. Save stalks for another use. Flowerets should be uniform in size (about 1 inch in diameter). Blanch broccoli in pasta water. When it is al dente, remove it from the water, transfer it to a bowl of ice water and drain thoroughly. If tuna or swordfish is fresh, poach it in a little water with white wine and lemon juice. Let fish cool and break into small chunks. Cook penne in salted, boiling water until al dente. Drain and rinse under cold running water until completely cooled, then drain completely. Put penne in large serving bowl. Add all remaining ingredients, except anchovies and olive oil. Heat olive oil in small pan over low heat. Cut anchovy fillets into small pieces, add to the olive oil and mash them with a fork until they dissolve. Do not let oil get too hot. Pour oil-anchovy mixture over salad, toss and serve immediately.

Serves 4-6

Minestra DiSalvo

In 1994, Mary DiSalvo became the last former resident to leave the old Greenbush neighborhood. She remembers the closeness of the ethnic settlement. Afterall, it had been her home since 1910 when she was born at 821 Regent Street to Angelo and Anne Masino, immigrants from Piana degli Albanesi, Sicily. The north side of the street, at 912 Regent Street, where she would reside later with her husband, Cosmo, had been spared during a 1960 urban renewal project. She remembers watching everything disappear before her eyes and wondered what they would do without the neighborhood and its people. When she decided, as a widow, to leave 30-some years later, it became yet another difficult time in her life. The area had embraced her since birth and it is never easy to leave friends behind. But by then, no one was left.

Featured in many Wisconsin State Journal cookbooks, Mary shared this family favorite, never before published.

1 medium onion, chopped into small pieces
Olive oil
One 10-ounce package of frozen artichoke hearts
One 10-ounce package of asparagus tips, or fresh asparagus tips, when in season
One 16-ounce can whole tomatoes, chopped, undrained
One 16-ounce can tiny early peas, undrained
Parsley
Sweet basil
1 pound ditalini (pasta)
Grated Parmesan or Romano cheese, optional.

Saute onion in small amount of olive oil. While still frozen, cut artichokes and asparagus into small pieces and cook as directed on packages. If using fresh asparagus tips, cook accordingly. Add to onion along with chopped tomatoes and juice. Season with freshly chopped parsley, basil, salt and pepper, to taste. In the meantime, boil water to cook pasta. When done, drain pasta, saving 1 cup hot water from pot to add to vegetable mixture. Add undrained can of peas just before serving. Mix with pasta

- and serve with grated cheese, if desired.

Note: The can of water is used to prevent vegetable mixture from becoming too dry. Use judgment as to the amount desired.

ROSE TROIA McCORMICK'S
CHEESE LASAGNA

This was served for years at Madison's beloved Paisan's restaurant, founded years ago by Roy McCormick and his wife, Rose Troia McCormick. It is yet another recipe Rose so kindly shared for both volumes of my Greenbush cookbooks.

1 pound lasagna noodles
Basic Tomato Sauce (see recipe, page 261)
FOR FILLING, BLEND TOGETHER:
1 pound fresh ricotta cheese
2 eggs
1 teaspoon salt
1/4 teaspoon pepper
1 Tablespoon parsley flakes
CHEESE FILLING:
1 cup shredded mozzarella cheese
2 cups shredded provolone cheese
1/2 cup grated Parmesan
Cook lasagna noodles al dente. Spread layer of Basic Tomato Sauce in a 9x13-inch baking pan. Arrange a layer of noodles, a layer of ricotta filling, a layer of shredded mozzarella and a layer of provolone and sauce. Repeat layers until all ingredients are used, ending with a layer of noodles topped with sauce and grated Parmesan cheese. Bake in a preheated oven at 375 degrees for 30 minutes.
Serves 8-12.

MEATLESS LASAGNA

The vegetarian lasagna recipe from an East Coast college commissary was not available, but Madisonian Isabel Hubbard offered her own low-fat meatless creation.

One (16-ounce) jar Healthy Choice spaghetti sauce, mushrooms added
2 cups low-fat mozzarella cheese
2 cups low-fat cottage cheese
1/2 cup grated low-fat Parmesan cheese
One (8- to 10-ounce) can stewed tomatoes
One (10-ounce) package frozen spinach, thawed and well-drained
1 teaspoon parsley flakes
1 teaspoon oregano flakes
1 package lasagna noodles, cooked

Spray a 9x12-inch pan with nonstick spray. Pour 1 cup spaghetti sauce on bottom of pan; place 3 to 4 lasagna noodles over sauce. Spread with half the mozzarella, cottage and grated Parmesan cheeses. Cover with entire package of thawed, well-drained spinach. Cover with sauce, stewed tomatoes and herbs. Add remaining noodles, cover with remaining sauce, add rest of cheese and cover with foil. Bake for 1 hour at 350 degrees. Let stand 15 minutes before cutting into squares to serve.

Makes 6 to 8 servings.

Note: Lasagna can be made the day ahead and easily reheated. Second-day servings will be firmer. Optional items can be added to the sauce, such as green pepper, zucchini, onions, mushrooms, etc.

TUNA LASAGNA

Here is a meatless dish in response to Ruth Boesel's request for tuna lasagna to serve at the next Boesel family gathering. It is deliciously different and a nice change from the traditional meat lasagna we've all grown to love.

1/2 pound lasagna noodles, cooked
2 Tablespoons butter or margarine
1/2 cup chopped onion
Two (6-ounce) cans water-packed tuna, drained
One (10+-ounce) can cream of mushroom soup
1/2 cup skim or whole milk
1/2 teaspoon garlic salt
1/2 teaspoon oregano
1/4 teaspoon pepper
1/4 teaspoon parsley flakes
1 1/2 cups cottage cheese
8 ounces mozzarella cheese, thinly sliced
1/4 cup grated Parmesan cheese

Heat oven to 350 degrees. Melt butter and saute onion. Add tuna, soup, milk and seasonings. Grease 7x11-inch baking dish. Place alternate layers of cooked noodles, tuna sauce, cottage cheese and sliced mozzarella, ending with the mozzarella. Sprinkle top with grated Parmesan. Bake 30 to 40 minutes. Cool 5 minutes before serving.

Yield: 6 large servings.

Merluzzo al Forno
Baked Cod

"Mamma" wouldn't part with the cod recipe she bakes each Friday in her northcentral Wisconsin restaurant, so I turned to Pasquale Bruno, Jr., well-known Chicago food columnist, teacher and cookbook author. His most recent book, "Italian, Light and Easy," was written with fat, cholesterol and calories in mind, without sacrificing flavor. This recipe is delicious and possibly better for you than what was remembered at "Mamma's"

2 Tablespoons virgin olive oil
1 Tablespoon finely chopped garlic
1/2 cup finely chopped yellow onion
1/4 cup chopped flat-leaf parsley
One (28-ounce) can plum tomatoes, with juice
1/4 cup chopped fresh basil or 1 teaspoon dried basil
1 teaspoon dried oregano, crumbled
1/2 teaspoon dried thyme, crumbled
4 to 5 grinds of black pepper
4 (5- to 6-ounce) cod fillets 3/4- to 1-inch thick

In a large nonreactive bowl, combine all ingredients except the fish. Leave at room temperature for 35 to 45 minutes to blend flavors. Preheat oven to 375 degrees. Place fish in a single layer in glass or porcelain baking dish. Pour sauce over fish. Bake for 20 to 25 minutes or until fish flakes gently when tested with a fork. To serve, place fillets on individual serving plates. Using slotted spoon, place some of the sauce over each fillet. Serve at once.

Makes 4 servings.
Calories: 243 per serving.

Boccone Dolce
(Sweet Mouthful)

Italians usually serve fresh fruit and cheese for dessert. About 20-some years ago I found this recipe in a local newspaper, tried it and fell hopelessly in love with it. By adding additional strawberries and toasted almonds, it became even more special.

9 large egg whites
2 cups sugar
1 teaspoon cream of tartar
1 1/2 teaspoons vanilla
9 ounces chocolate chips
4 Tablespoons water
1 1/2 pints whipping cream
1 tablespoon confectioners' sugar
1 quart fresh strawberries
Toasted almond slices, optional

Preheat oven to 450 degrees. Beat egg whites until stiff. Gradually add sugar, cream of tartar and vanilla. Butter a 9-by-13-inch pan. Pour in egg white mixture. Bake 2 minutes, then turn off oven and keep it closed until oven is cool. This can be baked at night and left in the oven until morning. Melt chocolate chips in water in double boiler. When cool, spread on top of baked egg white mixture. Whip cream; add 1 tablespoon confectioners' sugar. Spread half of this on top of the chocolate. Top with strawberries, reserving a few for garnish, then rest of whipped cream. Decorate with remaining strawberries and toasted almond slices. Refrigerate until ready to serve.

Serves 16 to 20.

Note: Amount of toasted almond slices can vary; however 1/4 to 1/2 cup works well. This is an optional ingredient and complements the dessert nicely.

Annie Stewart, Annie's Bed and Breakfast.

Breakfast
at the Inn

. . . . ●

THERE ARE NOT ENOUGH FINGERS ON ONE'S HANDS
TO COUNT THE MANY PLEASURES OF MADISON.
Recognized as one of America's finest cities, Madison has received
many honors lately that merely reinforce what old-timers knew for
years and what newcomers unwrap each day. The city is a treasure
chest of precious gifts, some obvious, others waiting to be
discovered. Back in 1855, Madison was having a "banner year." It
welcomed newspaper editor Horace Greeley as a visiting lecturer,
then savored his words of praise. In fact, it was a very good year.
Streets became lighted with gas; 350 buildings were erected; and
the population neared the 7,000 mark.

Greeley's description of what would become - and still is - the
only isthmus city in North America as "the most magnificent site of
any inland town" was sweet music to locals. The railroad in town
was celebrating its first birthday, and the University of Wisconsin
graduated its first class of . . . two. If one were to select Madison's
most shining attribute in 1993, it would most certainly begin with
the surrounding lakes that so impressed Greeley. What extends
outward from the shorelines are welcome additional gifts, many of
which have been protected through the years by concerned citizens,
nature lovers and the city Parks Division. One such amenity is
Warner Park, a 271-acre preserve situated on the city's far
Northeast Side that includes property once owned, cherished and
farmed by the Sachtjen and Bruns families. The farms were a blend
of splendid butternut and hickory nut trees scattered in all
directions, serving up an abundance of winter food for squirrels
and flavorful ingredients for holiday baking. Northern pike were
speared in collective waters that flowed from a lake inlet, and the
flat land beyond became perfect for pitched tents when the circus

came to town. There remains a hint of yesterday along the park's trails where pastures and silos once were, and the park's layout urges one to surrender to the seasonal splendor and tranquility. If you need convincing, ask Annie Stewart, proprietor of Madison's first bed and breakfast, called, appropriately, Annie's Bed & Breakfast. She is a lovely park blossom in her own right. Stewart's home on Sheridan Drive hugs a hill overlooking Warner Park and opens its arms to weary travelers and those yearning to make a connection with nature. It is also the site Blaine Sachtjen, as a child, referred to as "Happy Hollow." Stewart has added her own labels to certain places in view, such as Great Heron Marsh, Red Fox Glen, Owl Woods, Warner Meadow and Sled Hill, each named for obvious reasons. She will tell you of the deer that wander into her back yard to taste the salt lick positioned near the gazebo, and of her recent sighting of two white swans. Nine years ago, Stewart opened her doors for the world to enjoy a special taste of the isthmus city and the inside-out of a park she "oversees." Although her home was constructed in the 1960s, it is a tasteful fusion of past and present and lends itself well to the surroundings, its history, and the wonderful aroma of homemade sweet breads that treat each visitor like family. Since muffins are somewhat of a bed and breakfast trademark, it seemed natural for me to take advantage of an Indian summer hour to thread my way through the turning trees and bushes of the park to Annie's front door to ask for a tour . . . and a recipe for lemon poppyseed muffins.

LEMON POPPYSEED MUFFINS–
ANNIE'S BED AND BREAKFAST,
MADISON

Warner Park and the property once farmed by early German immigrants is just a fragment of what awaits visitors to Annie Stewart's bed and breakfast in Madison's northeast neighborhood of Brentwood Village. Lemon poppyseed muffins are one of the inn's many rewards.

2 cups all-purpose flour
3 Tablespoons grated fresh lemon peel
1/4 teaspoon salt
1 teaspoon baking powder
3 Tablespoons poppyseeds
1/4 pound (1 stick) very soft butter (not melted)
3/4 cup granulated sugar
1 Tablespoon pure lemon extract
2 large eggs, beaten, at room temperature
3/4 cup light sour cream
GLAZE:
Juice of one lemon
1/4 cup sugar

Mix together flour, lemon peel, salt, baking powder and poppyseed. Set aside. In another bowl, beat butter and 3/4 cup sugar until light and fluffy. Add extract, beaten eggs and sour cream; mix well.

Carefully fold into the dry ingredients. Do not overbeat. Fill buttered Pyrex muffin cups 2/3 full. Mixture will be nice and thick. Put cups on cookie sheet and bake in 400 degree oven until toothpick comes out clean. This time will vary from 15 to 25 minutes. Mix together glaze ingredients and heat until sugar melts. After muffins have baked, put some glaze on each muffin in their Pyrex cup. Let muffins cool in cups until ready to serve.

Note: If you prefer not to use Pyrex baking cups, muffins can be baked in buttered regular muffin tins. Yield will depend on container(s) used, 8 large or 16 small muffins.

Pumpkin Chocolate Chip Muffins

Linda Derrickson's Sunporch Cafe prepares and bakes; this favorite of Debbie Payne. Guests at the University Heights B & B also enjoy them for breakfast.

2 1/2 cups all-purpose flour
1 1/2 cups sugar
1/2 teaspoon baking powder
1 1/2 teaspoons baking soda
1 1/2 Tablespoons cinnamon
2 teaspoons nutmeg
2 teaspoons ginger
1/2 teaspoon ground cloves
1/2 teaspoon salt
3 extra-large eggs
1 1/2 cups mashed cooked pumpkin or squash
3/4 cup salad oil
3/4 cup semisweet chocolate chips

Combine dry ingredients in large, shallow mixing bowl. In another bowl, whisk together eggs, pumpkin or squash, and salad oil.

Add remaining ingredients to the dry mixture. Mix by hand until all flour is absorbed, adding chocolate chips while folding. Do not overmix. Scoop into greased muffin tins or foil liners and bake at 325 degrees until muffins spring back when lightly touched.

Unversity Club Basic Muffin

This campus landmark makes quality and quantity muffins flavored with Wisconsin grown fruit.

10 cups flour
5 cups sugar
1 Tablespoon baking powder
1 Tablespoon baking soda

Mix these ingredients. Make well in center and add: 10 eggs; 1 quart buttermilk; 2 cups salad oil. Mix all ingredients by hand just until dry ingredients are moist. Chopped, canned (drained), frozen or seasonal fruit can be added at the last mixing. Bake in greased or sprayed muffin tins at 350 degrees for 20 to 25 minutes.

Makes 5 to 6 dozen.

Note: Mix can be refrigerated several days before baking.

Quivey's Grove
Blueberry Muffins

Lynne Robertson, Middleton, didn't realize how delicious muffins could be until she tasted the blueberry muffins served in a basket during dinner at the old fieldstone mansion of Quivey's Grove on Nesbitt Road.

4 cups flour

1 cup sugar

2 teaspoons baking soda

1 teaspoon baking powder

1/4 teaspoon nutmeg

Dash of salt

1/4 pound margarine

2 eggs

2 cups buttermilk

1 1/2 cups blueberries

Preheat oven to 350 degrees. Grease large muffin cups. Sift flour, sugar, soda, baking powder, nutmeg and salt. Set aside. Melt butter. In large bowl, crack eggs and mix. Add buttermilk and mix. Add melted butter and mix. In two steps, add dry ingredients and mix lightly, just to moisten. Carefully fold in berries. Scoop into muffin tins. Sprinkle with sugar. Bake approximately 20 minutes or until done.

Makes 1 1/2 to 2 dozen.

French Pancakes

Filled with cottage cheese, jam or jelly, rolled up and dusted with confectioners' sugar, these become the breakfast treat Elizabeth Shuck remembers her stepmother making for her when Shuck was young.

1 cup flour
1/2 teaspoon salt
1 1/2 cups milk
3 eggs, well beaten

Sift flour and salt and add milk and eggs, beating together very well. Heat small skillet; grease slightly; pour in a little batter, tilt pan back and forth so batter will spread all over bottom. When brown, turn and brown on other side. Spread each pancake with jelly or cottage cheese and roll up and dust with confectioners' sugar. Serve hot.

Note: Pancakes may be browned on one side; place desired filling on browned side and roll. Set aside. When ready to serve, brown lightly.

BUTTERMILK WAFFLES
BOTTICELLI'S

Mary Bleecker, Sun Prairie calls these the best waffles in town. Owner Janie Capito was kind enough to share her recipe enjoyed by many each day at Botticelli's on King Streat near the Capital Square.

1 2/3 cups unsifted flour, leveled off
4 teaspoons baking powder
1/2 teaspoon salt
4 large eggs
2 cups buttermilk
12 to 16 Tablespoons melted butter

Blend dry ingredients. Add egg and milk. Mix with fork, then add butter, but do not overmix. Preheat waffle iron until very hot Add 1/2 cup batter for each waffle.

Belgian Waffles

After a reader asked for a Belgian waffle recipe, I decided to visit a few popular breakfast spots in town. Told more than once that they use just a regular waffle recipe, I searched further and found this recipe in the "Pancakes and Waffles" cookbook by Beatrice Ojakangas.

2 cups all-purpose flour
2 Tablespoons sugar
1/2 teaspoon nutmeg
1/4 teaspoon salt
1 cup milk
1 cup whipping cream
5 eggs, separated, and at room temperature
1/4 cup melted butter.

Preheat waffle iron. Combine dry ingredients in large bowl. Beat milk, cream, egg yolks and butter together. Stir into dry ingredients just until moistened. Whip egg whites until stiff. Fold into batter just until blended. Ladle into iron and cook until steam stops, about 3 to 5 minutes. If serving a crowd, waffles can be kept warm in oven. Nice served with strawberries, whipped cream, or just butter and maple syrup.

Makes three large waffles.

PRUNE BREAD

Janice Christensen's mother used to make a prune bread she described as almost black. This recipe was another favorite of Wheaton, Ill., school principal Edith Lewis, shared by Sandra Levin.

1/2 pound dried prunes
3/4 cup boiling water
1 3/4 cups flour
3/4 cup white sugar
1/2 teaspoon salt
1 teaspoon baking soda
1 egg
2 Tablespoons melted shortening

Soak prunes in cold water for 2 hours; drain. Pit prunes, cut fine; add boiling water. Let stand 5 minutes. Sift together flour, sugar, salt and baking soda and add to prune mixture. Beat egg and add to prune batter. Then add shortening. Pour into greased loaf pan. Bake at 325 degrees for about an hour or until tested done.

FRENCH BREAKFAST PUFFS

Nancy Kreklow, New Glarus, thought the recipe she had clipped from a farm magazine and used for years was lost forever.

1/3 cup butter or margarine

1/2 cups sugar

1 egg

1 1/2 cup flour

1 1/2 teaspoon baking powder

1/4 teaspoon salt

1/4 teaspoon nutmeg

1/2 cup milk

6 Tablespoons butter, melted

1/2 cup sugar

1 teaspoon cinnamon

Mix together butter, sugar and egg. Sift together dry ingredients, then add alternately with milk to the butter-sugar-egg mixture. Fill greased muffin tins 2/3 full. Bake at 375% for 20-25 minutes or until golden brown. Roll immediately in 6 Tablespoons melted butter, then coat with 1/2 cup sugar and 1 teaspoon cinnamon. Serve hot.

RHUBARB COFFEE CAKE

This is just another one of the many special items available at the Sunporch Cafe on University Avenue.

4 1/2 cups all-purpose flour
2 1/4 cups white sugar
1 1/2 teaspoons baking powder
2 1/4 teaspoons baking soda
1 cup butter
6 eggs
1 1/2 cups buttermilk (see note)
1 1/2 teaspoons vanilla
2 cups chopped rhubarb (other fruit can be substituted such as peaches, blueberries or apples)
STREUSEL MIXTURE:
1/4 cup brown sugar
1 cup all-purpose flour
2 teaspoons cinnamon
2 Tablespoons butter or margarine

Preheat oven to 350 degrees. Grease and flour a 9x13-inch standard cake pan. Mix flour, sugar, baking powder, baking soda and 1 cup butter to a fine meal.

Whisk together eggs, buttermilk and vanilla. Add to dry ingredients. Mix until just combined. Do not overmix. Spread 1/2 of the batter in pan. Combine streusel ingredients until crumbly. Mix 1/2 the streusel mixture with 2 cups of chopped rhubarb (or other fruit of choice) and layer this on top of the batter. Add remaining batter to pan. Top with remaining streusel. Bake at 350 degrees for 45-60 minutes.

Note: If buttermilk is unavailable, substitute 1 1/2 tablespoons vinegar in milk to make 1 1/2 cups total. If a heart-healthy version is desired, use Eggbeaters and soy margarine or oil. If oil is used, increase flour by 1/2 cup.

Southwestern Sausage and Cheese Casserole

The First Place winner in a 1994 Country Living magazine contest serves 12 and is perfect for brunch anytime of the year.

Two (7-ounce) or four (4-ounce) cans chopped mild green chilies

6 corn tortillas, cut into 1/2inch strips

1 pound bulk hot Italian sausage, cooked and drained

2 cups shredded Monterey Jack cheese

1/2 cup milk

8 large eggs

1/2 teaspoon each of salt, garlic salt, onion salt, ground cumin and ground black pepper

2 large ripe tomatoes, sliced

Paprika; Light sour cream, optional

Prepared salsa, optional

Grease a 9x13-inch baking dish. Layer half of chilies, tortilla strips, sausage and cheese. Repeat with remaining chilies, tortilla strips, sausage and cheese. In medium bowl, beat a with fork milk, eggs and seasonings until well mixed; pour over casserole. Arrange tomato slices on top. Sprinkle with paprika. Cover with plastic wrap and refrigerate overnight.

Next day, heat oven to 325 degrees. Remove plastic wrap and bake 45 to 55 minutes or until center and edges are slightly browned. Serve with sour cream and salsa, if desired.

CRUSTLESS QUICHE

An Egg Beater favorite of Stoughton resident Pat Smith.

1 small zucchini, sliced (about 1 cup)
1 cup sliced carrots
1/2 cup chopped onion
1/2 cup diced red pepper
2 Tablespoons margarine
1 cup cracker meal
1 teaspoon baking powder
1/8 to 1/4 teaspoon ground red pepper
1 (8-ounce) carton Egg Beaters
1 1/2 cups skim milk

In nonstick skillet, over medium heat, cook zucchini, carrots, onion and red pepper in 1 teaspoon margarine until tender, stirring occasionally. Spoon mixture into lightly greased 9-inch pie plate. In bowl, combine cracker meal, baking powder and ground red pepper; cut in remaining 5 teaspoons margarine until mixture resembles coarse crumbs. Whisk in Egg Beaters and milk until well blended. Pour over vegetable mixture. Bake at 400 degrees for 30 minutes or until puffed and golden. Let stand 5 minutes before serving.

Makes 6 servings.

No-Crust Quiche

Featured in the Wisconsin State Journal in 1985, this quiche was clipped and used many times by Paula Flaig down in Lisle, Illinois. When she misplaced it, Margie Schilt, Monroe, came to the rescue.

One (9 ounce) package frozen broccoli spears
1 small onion, chopped
1 green pepper, chopped
1 cup shredded cheddar cheese
1/2 cup shredded Swiss cheese
1 1/2 cups milk
4 eggs
1 teaspoon salt
1/4 teaspoon pepper
3/4 cup biscuit mix
1 cup diced ham

Heat oven to 400 degrees. Grease quiche pan or a 9-inch cake pan. Cut broccoli into bite-size pieces; combine with other vegetables and cheese in pan. Beat together remaining ingredients until smooth, and pour into pan. Bake 35 to 40 minutes. Let stand 5 minutes before serving.

Yield: 6 to 8 servings

Note: Schilt prefers using chopped frozen broccoli and, instead of cheddar and Swiss, Velveeta cheese.

My sister, Elaine Tripalin,
with a basket filled with Girl
Scout Cookies in front of
Lowell School – mid 1940s.

Cookie Jar

. . . . ●

ONE BITE OF THE THIN, ROUND, CRISP GINGER
COOKIE AND I BECAME A LITTLE GIRL ONCE AGAIN.
A dark green tam covered part of my French braids and the yellow
scarf worn under my collar, secured by a knot decorated with a
goldlike three-leaf clover pin, complemented my green uniform.

It was the mid-1940s and Girl Scout cookie selling time.
Madisonians could purchase delicious ginger cookies from girls
who ran house-to-house ringing doorbells throughout the city.
Packaged by the dozen in wax paper bags and selling for 50 cents,
the cookies were like Red Dot potato chips. You couldn't eat just
one. This annual treat, baked by Strand's Bakery on Atwood
Avenue near Schenk's Corner, was so popular that households often
purchased five to 10 dozen. And, at 50 cents a bag, it was easy to
add, subtract and give back change. For all the heartbreak that
accompanied World War II, there was still a smile behind every
door, making cookie time fun for everyone.

When I opened a letter from Pat Hart, Monona, little did I
realize that her request would tug hard at my heartstrings. Longing
for one of the Girl Scout cookies from childhood days, Hart
wondered if I could locate the recipe. I knew if I could, it would
please not only Hart and me, but half of Madison as well, for if
anyone had the pleasure of eating one of those cookies with a tall
glass of cold milk, a secured recipe would become an overnight
treasure.

Madison's chapter of the Madison Council of Girl Scouts was
established in 1927 with an initial membership of 236. They
experienced tremendous growth during the 1930s and 1940s and
by 1954, with a membership of more than 4,000, the council
changed its name to Black Hawk in honor of the famous Indian

chief. In search of a good cookie for Scouts to sell as a fund-raiser, a recipe was selected from the collection of Mrs. Frank Kessenich Sr. It would remain the cookie baked and sold for years until the demand became overwhelming.

Esther Gandt, 86, a former leader, trainer and board member, contacted me with "Grandma Kessenich's" original family-size recipe used before adaption for commercial baking. Another response arrived from Nancy Hutson with the same recipe, this one given to her by a former board member, Mrs. Elbert H. Carpenter, and found in the 1958 publication of the Black Hawk Council Cookbook. A third response states that the original Kessenich recipe had been taken through its initial stages by Girl Scout Director Esther Williams.

But the recipe that intrigued me most was one sent by Dorothy Kruse on an index card, a bit yellowed with age, that read: Strand Bakery Girl Scout Cookies. Kruse didn't remember where the card came from, but I just had to try it. That's when my taste buds lit up and I became a Girl Scout once again in Mrs. Derra's 1940-something St. Bernard's Girl Scout Troop. Brothers Trygve and Reidar Strand baked thousands of these magnificent cookies through the years and we are all delighted to share this nostalgic cookie recipe with you.

Strand Bakery
Girl Scout cookies

1 cup brown sugar
1 cup white sugar
1 cup shortening
2 eggs
1/3 cup dark molasses
1 teaspoon baking soda, dissolved in 1 Tablespoon boiling water and allowed to cool
Sift together:
3 1/2 cups flour
2 teaspoons baking soda
1 teaspoon salt
1 Tablespoon cinnamon
1/2 teaspoon ginger
Blend in order given. Chill and roll 1/8-inch thick.

Cut out with round cookie cutter. Sprinkle with sugar and water to form cracks. Bake at 400 degrees for 10 minutes or 375 degrees for 12 minutes. Need not grease pan, but remove quickly.

Note: Instead of rolling out dough and using cookie cutter, chill dough, then roll into walnut-sized balls, pressing each down with a glass dipped in sugar. Sprinkling with water is not necessary. These should bake to about 3 inches in diameter, so space dough accordingly. Bake at 375 degrees. Additional sprinkling of sugar can be added upon removal from oven. Cool on rack and store in tight-lidded glass or tin container.

Grandma Kessenich's Spice Cookies

Esther Gandt, former Girl Scout leader, trainer and board member, shared this original family-sized recipe before adaptation for commercial baking.

1 cup granulated sugar
1 egg
2 teaspoons ginger
2 teaspoons cinnamon
4 Tablespoons cold water
1 cup shortening
1 cup molasses
1 teaspoon baking soda
3 1/2 cups flour

Mix and chill in refrigerator. Roll very thin and sprinkle with sugar. Bake at 375 degrees for approximately 7 minutes or until done.

Note: Suggestions are to add more flour for a better dough and to roll as thin as possible. Another suggestion is to chill dough overnight, then roll into balls and press with bottom of a glass dipped in sugar. Additional sprinkling of sugar is optional.

Coconut Kisses

One of my own favorites from childhood days. I could never eat just one.

2 egg whites
1 cup sugar
1 teaspoon vanilla
Dash of salt
2 cups cornflakes
1 cup shredded coconut
1/2 cup chopped nuts

Beat egg whites until stiff. Fold in remaining ingredients and drop by tablespoonfuls on lightly greased and floured cookie sheet. Bake at 300 degrees about 20 minutes. Remove when light golden brown.

Coconut Macaroons

Printed many years ago on cans of condensed milk, this coconut macaroon recipe became an instant hit. Although Ruby Ferge made them many times, she couldn't remember the exact ingredients and amounts. Many readers responded.

2/3 cup Eagle Brand sweetened condensed milk
2 2/3 cups flaked coconut
1 teaspoon vanilla extract
3/4 teaspoon almond extract

In medium-size bowl, combine all ingredients until well blended. Drop by teaspoonful, about 1-inch apart onto well-greased baking sheet. Bake in 350 degree oven, eight to 10 minutes, or until lightly browned. Immediately remove from baking sheet. Cool.

Makes about 1 1/2 dozen 1 1/2-inch diameter cookies.

MELT-IN-YOUR-MOUTH SUGAR COOKIES

A 1952 4-H cookbook winner and all-time favorite of Stoughton resident Pat Smith, Stoughton.

1 cup Crisco
1 cup white sugar
1 cup powdered sugar
1 cup vegetable oil
2 eggs
4 1/4 cups all-purpose flour
1 teaspoon salt
1 teaspoon cream of tartar
1 teaspoon baking soda
1 teaspoon vanilla
Sugar and nutmeg for dipping the glass in to flatten cookies

Cream Crisco, sugars and oil together in large mixing bowl. Add eggs and beat until smooth. Add flour, salt, cream of tartar, soda and vanilla. Mix well. Combine sugar and nutmeg in a separate dish to tip glass for flattening cookies. Form cookie dough into walnut-size balls and place on greased cookie sheet. Flatten cookies with a glass dipped in sugar-nutmeg mixture. Bake at 375 degrees for 8 to 10 minutes. Cool. Makes about five dozen cookies.

Note: On occasion, Smith has used 5 cups of flour.

Sugar Cookies

Meg Ford used to make this basic cookie for her children, but recently misplaced the recipe. Tom DiSalvo answered the call with help from his 1942 "Good Housekeeping Cookbook."

3/4 cup granulated sugar
1/2 cup melted shortening or salad oil
2 eggs, beaten
1 teaspoon vanilla extract
2 cups sifted all-purpose flour
1 teaspoon cream of tartar
1/2 teaspoon baking soda
1/2 teaspoon salt

Blend sugar well with shortening. Stir in beaten eggs and vanilla. Sift flour, cream of tartar, baking soda and salt; add to shortening mixture gradually while mixing well. Chill until easy to handle. Then turn out onto lightly floured board. Roll to 1/8-inch thickness, then cut with floured 3-inch scalloped cutter. Arrange cookies on a greased baking sheet, about 2 inches apart. Sprinkle with granulated sugar and cinnamon, if desired. Bake at 375 degrees for 10-12 minutes.

Makes about 1 1/2 to 2 dozen cookies.

PASTEL COOKIES

Perfect for anytime, but especially when celebrations beg for varieties of colors and flavors...

3 1/2 cups all-purpose flour
1 teaspoon baking powder
1 1/2 cups butter or margarine
1 cup sugar
1 package (3 oz.) Jell-O, any flavor
1 egg
1 teaspoon vanilla

Mix flour with baking powder. Cream butter; gradually add sugar and gelatin, beating well. Beat in egg and vanilla. Gradually add flour mixture, mixing well. Force dough through cookie press onto ungreased baking sheets. Sprinkle with additional gelatin (same flavor). Decorate, if desired. Bake at 400 degrees about 8 minutes, or until edges are golden brown. Makes about 10 dozen 1- to 1 1/2-inch cookies.

OLD-FASHIONED OATMEAL RAISIN COOKIES

As a member of the Two Rivers 4-H Club in Webster, Wis., eleven year old Travis Gravesen entered his favorite cookies in the 1994 Burnett County Fair and returned home to the family farm that evening with the Purple Ribbon Best of Show honors.

The recipe's origin is the "Pillsbury Best Cookbook."

1 cup raisins
2 cups all-purpose flour
1 teaspoon soda
1 teaspoon salt
1/2 teaspoon nutmeg
1 teaspoon cinnamon
1/4 teaspoon ground cloves
1 cup shortening (Travis uses butter-flavored Crisco)
1 cup sugar
2 eggs
1 teaspoon vanilla extract
2 cups quick oatmeal
1 cup chopped walnuts

Place raisins in small saucepan and cover with water. Simmer 10 minutes. Drain and reserve 1/3 cup of raisin liquid. Cool. Mix dry ingredients. Gradually blend sugar and shortening and cream until light and fluffy. Blend egg and vanilla. Stir in raisins and liquid. Add sifted dry ingredients and rolled oats and nuts. Mix thoroughly and drop by rounded teaspoonfuls onto ungreased cookie sheet. Bake at 375 degrees for 10 to 12 minutes.

CHOCOLATE CREAM DROPS

Karen Slaght's mother often placed a large marshmallow half, cut side down, on top of each cookie as soon as they were removed from the oven. When cooled, she frosted them with a chocolate glaze. This recipe is from a sour cream cookbook purchased at the 1960 Iowa State Fair.

1/2 cup butter

Two 1-ounce squares unsweetened chocolate, melted

1 1/2 cups sugar

2 eggs

1 cup sour cream

1 teaspoon vanilla

2 3/4 cups flour

1/2 teaspoon baking soda

1/2 teaspoon baking powder

1/2 teaspoon salt

1 cup chopped nuts

large marshmallows, optional

chocolate frosting, optional

Cream butter and add chocolate. Gradually add sugar. Beat in eggs, one at a time, then add sour cream and vanilla. Sift flour, soda, baking powder and salt; gradually add to mixture. Add nuts. Chill at least one hour. Drop rounded teaspoonfuls about two inches apart on lightly greased cookie sheet. Bake at 375 degrees for 10 minutes.

Cherry Winks

When Norma Narf requested this recipe, I had no idea what the response would be. As the Junior First Prize Winner in Pillsbury's Second Grand National Baking contest held in 1950, cherry winks quickly became a household favorite, thanks to Ruth Derousseau, Rice Lake, Wis.

2 1/4 cups sifted all-purpose flour
1 teaspoon baking powder
1/2 teaspoon baking soda
1/2 teaspoon salt
3/4 cup butter
1 cup sugar
2 unbeaten eggs
2 Tablespoons milk
1 teaspoon vanilla
1 cup chopped pecans
1 cup chopped dates
1/3 cup drained and chopped maraschino cherries
2 1/2 cups crushed cornflakes
Maraschino cherry slices for garnish

Preheat oven to 375 degrees. Sift together dry ingredients and set aside. Cream butter and gradually add sugar, creaming well. Add eggs, milk and vanilla and beat well. Blend in dry ingredients gradually and mix thoroughly. Add nuts, dates and cherries and mix well. If desired, chill dough before shaping. Drop by rounded teaspoonfuls into crushed cornflakes, toss lightly to coat, then shape into balls. Place on greased baking sheets and top each with a slice of maraschino cherry. Bake for 12 to 15 minutes.

Makes about 5 dozen cookies.

Clara Gulseth (left) with unidentified employee at the Ice Cream Shop
across from East High on East Washington Avenue.

High school hangouts

· •

ACCORDING TO JERRY MINNICH'S WISCONSIN
ALMANAC (NORTH COUNTRY PRESS), ON THE FIRST
DAY OF AUTUMN THE SUN WILL RISE IN THE TRUE
EAST AND SET IN THE TRUE WEST, AND DAY AND
NIGHT WILL BE EQUAL LENGTH EVERYWHERE ON
EARTH. We all know that everything preceding or following that
day is a toss-up. As a fickle month, September can't seem to make up
its mind if it should prolong the heat of August or get a jump on the
crispness of October.

Also found in the almanac is a monthly list of record-breaking
days dating from the 1880s. I noticed that on Sept. 9, 1955, as I was
entering my senior year at East High School, the temperature soared
to 97 degrees. You can bet we suffered wearing our new wool skirts
and sweaters the first week of school, despite the heat. Our only relief
was having Harold Cnare's Ice Cream Shop across the street from
East High. Cnare's affair with ice cream began in 1931 when he and
his wife, Eleanor, went into business with Eleanor's father, John
Ahrens, and his brother, Fred, about a block from West High School
on Regent Street. Nestled between Look Pharmacy, Jerry Emmerich's
Grocery Store and Hegerich Bakery, the shop became so popular that
in 1945 Harold Cnare decided to purchase Bassett's Ice Cream Shop
on East Washington Avenue, just a hop, skip, and jump across the
street from East High.

Marian Douglas, Cnare's daughter, reflects back on the hard work
involved. But she also remembers that everything was laced with
good times, as well. Working 60 hours each week peeling bananas
and peaches by the bushel and hulling mountains of strawberries for
fresh fruit ice cream, she also waited on customers and still got her
homework done. There was the refreshing pink peppermint ice

cream made with crushed peppermints leftover from Christmas; the tin roof sundaes of vanilla ice cream drizzled with chocolate sauce, malted milk powder and sprinkled with salty peanuts as a garnish; the famous "Round the World" banana splits; and the best malted milk ice cream around, made with Hershey and Horlick products. And never to be forgotten was Cnare's new invention– frozen malt served fresh from a machine that intrigued all of Madison and its periphery.

For four years, my friends chose to eat every lunch at the ice cream shop rather than the school cafeteria. "Lunch hour" was a misnomer because we had only enough time to run across the street, place our purses and books in "our" booth, stand in line to order a soda, french fries, sloppy joe or hamburger, and a piece of Bjelde's pie for dessert, eat fast, then get back to school before afternoon classes began. The crew of employees had just enough time to recuperate from us before the next shift of kids arrived. There was a repeat of ice cream cones and sodas, malted milks and sundaes ordered after school when there was more time to spend with friends, and time to make each spoonful or strawful a melting moment to savor

The ladies who worked at Cnare's were like everyone's mom, especially Clara Gulseth, who tucked away 35 years as an employee with a smile for everyone and a belief that each young customer was special. With Harold and Eleanor as overseers, the ice cream shop was home away from home, squeaky clean and so much fun to be a part of.

The demise of Cnare's began when the old, "tough" and seemingly grouchy principals were replaced with new free-thinking leaders who loosened the rigid standards of academia for those not interested in school. The jukebox no longer played Elvis and Doris Day tunes and saddle shoes and pressed wash pants were replaced with worn-out tennis shoes and torn jeans. School officials had always supplied Cnare with an honor roll so he would know who was allowed out of study hall during school hours. But the communication halted, and cooperation came to a standstill. Cnare's shop became so burdened with "skippers" that he was forced to lock the door during school hours. The truants pounded on the door and glass windows until one day, after being threatened, Cnare decided he had had enough and locked the doors forever. I was glad when brothers Dick and Bob Trameri asked me to find the recipe for the Ice Cream Shop's Sloppy Joes, also known as "Beefers." It meant making a connection with people who made the good teen years even better for me.

240

'Beefers' – Harold Cnare's Ice Cream Shop

We didn't have much time to eat during lunch hour, but these were quick and delicious. 'Beefers' were destined to become a part of life for many students at East and West High Schools, and it's a sure bet that most of the students who enjoyed them back then wish they could slide into a booth at the old Ice Cream Shop for one more taste.

5 pounds ground beef
2 medium onions, chopped
1 (24-ounce) can tomato soup
1 cup catsup
1/4 cup Worcestershire sauce
Salt and pepper

Brown meat and chopped onions. Add remaining ingredients. Simmer, being careful not to burn. Makes a lot, but easily frozen.

Note: To make the well-remembered Ice Cream Shop chili, use this recipe, add chili powder, kidney beans and a can of stewed tomatoes. After a "beefer," there was always room left for a hot fudge sundae.

SPANISH HAMBURGERS, HAROLD CNARE'S ICE CREAM SHOP

The women in the neighborhood would bring glass jars to the Ice Cream Shop on Friday to take home any leftover Spanish hamburger sauce. On Sundays Cnare would begin preparing a new batch of sauce for the busy week ahead.

2 quarts water
Two (20-ounce bottles) Heinz catsup (recommended brand)
2 large onions, chopped
1/4 cup celery salt, or to taste
Salt and pepper
Red pepper, to taste
2 Tablespoons chili powder

Put all ingredients in roaster and simmer 2-3 hours. Fry 100 hamburgers and place burgers in roaster and refrigerate overnight. The next day, reheat and serve burgers with a little juice.

Makes 100.

Serve hot for sandwiches on bread or buns.

Note: If using ground chuck, there will be little or no grease in filling. However, if using ground beef, any grease that remains in cooked mixture can be easily removed with a spoon.

Hot Fudge Sauce, Harold Cnare's Ice Cream Shop

1 (14-ounce) can evaporated milk
2 Tablespoons butter
1/4 pound unsweetened cocoa
Dash salt
1 1/3 cups white sugar
1 teaspoon vanilla

Bring milk and butter to boil; add cocoa, sugar and salt and stir. Remove from burner and add vanilla. Continue to stir until smooth, or whir in blender. Ready to serve. This recipe can be tripled. Store in refrigerator.

SPUDNUTS

Like Red Dot Potato Chips, who could east just one? We munched on Spudnuts while we walked, talked, sat during football games at Breese Stevens, gathered after the LOFT, then, if there were some left over, munched again for breakfast after slumber parties. Carried out of a Spudnut Shop in a white paper bag, each dougnut was savored, bite for bite. A few years ago, brothers Tom and Rod Shaugnessy were reminiscing their teen years and wondered if I could find the recipe for Nibblenook hamburgers and Spudnuts. I have yet to write what I learned about the hamburgers, but in the meantime, Dorothy McCluskey, Spring Green, mailed the recipe for the spudnuts she has been making since clipping the recipe in 1966 from a Farm Journal and Farmer's Wife magazine. She described them as welcome treats when her kids came home from school. Later, dozens would find a way to reach college dorms. McCluskey assures me that her freezer always has an ample supply for anyone who happens to arrive at the house. . . hungry.

This isn't the same doughnut Tom and Rod Shaugnessy remember, but I hope it is a close second.

1 3/4 cups milk
1/2 cup shortening
1/2 cup sugar
1/2 cup mashed potatoes
2 packages active dry yeast
1/2 cup warm water (105 to 115 degrees)
2 eggs, beaten
1/2 teaspoon vanilla
6 1/2 to 7 cups flour
1 teaspoon baking powder
2 teaspoons salt

Scald milk and shortening, stir in sugar and mashed potatoes. Cool to lukewarm (90 degrees). Blend well. Sprinkle yeast over warm water and stir until yeast is dissolved. Add to lukewarm mixture. Stir in beaten eggs and vanilla. Sift 6 1/2 cups flour with baking powder and salt; add gradually to lukewarm mixture. Mix well after each addition. Add another 1/2 cup sifted flour if needed. (This is a soft dough.) Turn into a greased container, cover and let rise until double in bulk, about 1 1/2 hours. On well-floured board, roll out dough to about 1/2-inch thickness. Cut with floured doughnut cutter. Place cut doughnuts on wax paper, cover with a cloth and let rise until double in bulk. Fry spudnuts, a few at a time, in melted shortening or oil heated to 375 degrees. Drain on absorbent paper. Makes about four dozen. If desired, they can be frosted or rolled in cinnamon and sugar.

Coney Island Chili Sauce— Noteses' State Street Coney Island

A high school or college student could never tire of State Street. Every block held a plethora of stimulation. Greek-owned Coney Island was located in the 300-block with the Notes family in command. Next door was "George's," owned by George Gerothanas, also of Greek ancestry. Both places were especially popular with Central High students, and other teenagers from East and West High who became friends as members of the LOFT on East Doty Street. Coney Islands, hamburgers and fries with a Coca-Cola or, if you had an extra quarter, a thick chocolate malt. Hours were spent on stools or in booths, just "hanging out" with good friends. Coney Island owner Tom Notes remembers well the good memories that began back in 1921. But he also remembers the anti-war demonstrations of the 1960s that created hurdles many State Street businesses could not clear. When the doors of Coney Island were locked for the last time, the spicy mouthwatering family sauce recipe that covered thousands of weiners in thousands of buns also became nothing more than a memory. . . the kind one never wants to forget.

15 pounds of hamburger
1 large onion, chopped fine, or to taste
1 box (about 1 pound) fine cracker meal
6 large spoonfuls of chili powder (see note)
6 large spoonfuls of paprika
6 large spoonfuls salt
2 large spoonfuls ground cumin seed
2 large spoonfuls celery salt
2 large spoonfuls garlic powder
Crisco

Brown onion and hamburger in Crisco. Add spices. Stir thoroughly to prevent sticking. Sprinkle cracker meal to cover mixture, then stir in enough water to form a thin

246

paste. Simmer for four hours. Freezes well.

Note: To make chili, add brown beans before simmering. The "large" spoonful is the stainless steel size used in commercial kitchens for stirring kettles of simmering ingredients.

"Maid-Rite" Sandwiches

A "loose" hamburger sandwich, created in Iowa back in the 1920s, has been satisfying the masses ever since, especially the teenagers. The recipe has never been shared, yet found in a Buchanan County, Iowa, Amish cookbook, is this recipe for "Maid-Rite" sandwiches. I cannot claim its authenticity, but it should suffice if you don't happen to have a Maid-Rite Sandwich Shop as we do, on Odana Road near West Towne Mall.

2 pounds of hamburger
1 cup of ketchup
2 onions, diced
1 teaspoon prepared mustard
1 teaspoon chili powder
Salt, to taste

Put raw hamburger and remaining ingredients in top of double boiler. Cook 1 hour.

Old menu from Baron's Tea Room.

Menus from
the past

. . . . •

EVERY NOW AND THEN, A ONCE-VIBRANT
BUSINESS DISTRICT SUCCUMBS TO AGE AND
NEGLECT, ONLY TO BE LATER REVITALIZED BY
PEOPLE WITH INSIGHT, FORTITUDE AND
DEDICATION. Removing tarnished appearances can be done
tactfully and tastefully with the cooperation of many until the area
takes on a new look without erasing building facades, cornerstones,
character and fond recollections. Such is the case with the area that
gently slopes from the Capitol Square to rest in the 400 and 500
blocks of East Wilson Street.

Its historical niche, overlooking Lake Monona, can be described
as having a lifetime of peaks and valleys, beginning with great
promise in the early 1900s, when the Chicago & North Western
Railway brought people to the depot (where Madison Gas and
Electric Co. is now) as an introduction to Madison. With the
Wilson and Cardinal Hotels being built at the same time to
accommodate visitors and newcomers alike, a potpourri of other
businesses sprouted, adding variety to a neighborhood that would
be known years later for its colorful past. Ida Browne remembers
some of the good times. It was during the 1940s when Browne,
then Ida McDonald, was hired as a waitress at the Cardinal Hotel
coffee shop. Located on the corner of East Wilson and Franklin
streets, the red brick hotel served some of the best food in town. It
was enjoyed by state employees as well as some of Madison's well-
known residents, including Art Schroeder of Schroeder Funeral
Home, the William Fauerbachs of Fauerbach Brewery, Perry and
Alice Fess of the Fess Hotel a few blocks away, and our beloved,
one-of-a-kind "Roundy" Coughlin, popular sportswriter for the
Wisconsin State Journal. Out-of-town celebrities visited, too,

- including baseball great Lou Gehrig, whose picture with Roundy, the manager of the St. Louis Cardinals, and Cardinal Hotel owner Art McCance, hung behind the hotel bar as a reminder of a trip to St. Louis and the World Series in the late 1920s. Homestyle roast beef, ham or chicken fricassee with dumplings was served on Sundays for $1. People lined up on the sidewalk for a meal that included homemade everything, from soup to dessert. During the week the menu boasted a 35 cent noon lunch with the sandwich of the day, soup, dessert and coffee. In the evening one could dine on steak and homemade hash browns for 55 cents and special items like freshly baked Cornish pasties. The person responsible for preparing the daily offerings was a short, robust woman named Helen Hval, who began each day at 6 a.m. making 30 pies, which would disappear before closing, then continue the pace until 8 p.m. with only a brief afternoon break. Some of the others who made up the Cardinal Hotel "family" were bartender Glenn "Brownie" Browne, who became Ida's husband; Virginia Grayson, who helped head desk clerk Harry Mirvis; and Molly, the part-time cook. One of the many heydays of the neighborhood took place during World War II when the bus stop in front brought soldiers from Truax Field for a weekend to hang out there as well as at the newly opened Hoffman House restaurant, where the Essen House is located today. Hval, known to all as Aunt Helen, caught few minutes of rest each day to sit at the kitchen table behind the scenes, otherwise scurrying from one side to the other, cooking from scratch. Of all the praise showered on her through the years, her French dressing probably took top honors. Customers would bring in jars to be filled for a quarter with the dressing that "never separated." Her recipe, made in large quantities in the hotel's mixmaster, was kept a secret until she died, at which time hotel owners Art and Ethel McCance passed it on to their waitresses.

CARDINAL HOTEL
FRENCH DRESSING

3/4 cup salad oil
6 teaspoons vinegar
1 teaspoon grated onion
Dash pepper
1 garlic clove
1/4 cup catsup
Mix very well in blender and refrigerate.

Note: This recipe was found by Armand P. Richman, Madison, in his deceased mother's card file. Written in longhand, it accompanied two other salad dressings, one labeled "Pine's," and the other, "Memorial Union." The authenticity of each one is unknown. One can only hope they are the secrets we have been waiting patiently for.

French Garlic Dressing

The Pine's Restaurant in Middleton was a popular restaurant that served juicy steaks, baked potatoes with sour cream and a French garlic dressing to remember forever. Although the former owner's family preferred to keep the recipe a secret, a handwritten card was found in Armand P. Richman's deceased mother's recipe box with "The Pine's" written in pencil. One can only assume the authenticity of this recipe, however Madisonian Carol Hird made it as soon as it was featured in my column and claims it is the "real thing." If you have a good memory of flavors, you be the judge. . .

1 onion, grated
2 garlic cloves, grated
1/2 cup vinegar
1/2 cup sugar
2 teaspoons paprika
1 cup salad oil
2 teaspoons salt
1 cup catsup
Mix in blender and refrigerate.

Aunt Helen's French Dressing– Cardinal Hotel Coffee Shop, circa 1940s

Can of tomato juice (about 23 ounces)
2 cups sugar
1 3/4 cups vinegar
3 cups salad oil
2 Tablespoons salt (approximately)
1/8 to 1/4 cup Worchestershire sauce
2 Tablespoons dry mustard
1 Tablespoon onion juice
1 1/8 teaspoon paprika

Mix very well in order given in an ample container.
Note: We have reduced this recipe from the original, which makes restaurant-size proportions, so some ingredients are approximate. Also, if you can't find onion juice in a grocery store, you can puree, then strain enough onion to make 1 tablespoon juice.

MEMORIAL UNION FRENCH DRESSING

Equal portions of each:
Vinegar
Chili sauce
Onions
Oil
Sugar (should be half the amount).
Mix very well and refrigerate.

Hot Bacon Dressing

Long time Madisonians remember the excitement generated in 1946 when seven Hoffman brothers opened a restaurant down at 514 East Wilson Street near the train depot. A salad bar, like a treasure chest of priceless jewels on display, quickly became the talk of the town. To this day, when I pass the Essen Haus, former Hoffman House location, my mind reverts back to the heels of World War II when the restaurant rose to fame overnight. This dressing is still used at the Hoffman House restaurant in Janesville, and was requested by Janesville resident, Winifred Quarg.

1/4 ounce au jus prep (beef boullion may be substituted)
1/4 pound onions, diced
1/4 pound bacon, chopped
1 cup water
1 cup vinegar
2/3 cup plus 1 Tablespoon sugar
1/4 teaspoon black pepper
3 to 4 Tablespoons cornstarch
1/4 cup water

Saute bacon and onions until brown. Pour off liquid and fat and reserve both. Heat 1 cup water, vinegar, sugar and pepper until boiling. Mix cornstarch with fat and liquid from bacon and onions to make a paste then add 1/4 cup water and au jus prep. Stir into vinegar/sugar mixture. Bring back to a boil and simmer 10 minutes. Then add bacon and onions. Remove from heat. Heating procedure is in double boiler until thoroughly heated.

Yields about 2 1/2 quarts.

Fragrant Oriental Shrimp and Vegetables

Chef Howard Bender, at one time the general manager of the "Ovens on Monroe Street" changed this soup recipe each time it was prepared.

1 1/2 cups rice wine vinegar (you can substitute white wine vinegar)
6 cups chicken broth
Crushed red peppers - season as spicy as you like
1 cup broccoli - cut into small pieces
1 cup carrots - cut into thin strips
1 cup bean sprouts
1 cup pea pods - just pick the ends
1/4 cup sweet red pepper - fine dice
2 cups baby bay shrimp
Cornstarch

Place vinegar in a pot and bring to a boil. Reserve 1/4 cup. Let boil until reduced in half. Add broth and crushed peppers. Bring to a boil again and add vegetables and shrimp. Simmer just until vegetables are cooked. Mix some cornstarch and vinegar together to make a light paste. With soup almost at a boil, slowly whisk in the paste until it thickens the broth. You are ready to eat. This soup will lose its texture if heated, chilled, and reheated again as the cornstarch breaks down, so eat and enjoy quickly!

Tanyeri Grill's Patlican Salatasi (Eggplant Salad)

Although the Tanyeri Grill is closed, owner Kamil Tanyeri shared these recipes from his former King Street location. They are reminders of a great menu and memorable dining experiences.

3 to 4 medium eggplants, peeled and cut into 1/2-inch slices
1/2 cup olive oil for grilling
2 Tablespoons tahini (sesame paste)
3 cloves garlic, minced
2 Tablespoons extra virgin olive oil
Juice of 1 lemon
Pinch of crushed red pepper
Salt and pepper, to taste
Fresh chopped parsley and lemon wedges, for garnish

Brush eggplant slices with olive oil. Grill over hot coals until well browned (almost black) on both sides, turning and brushing with more olive oil as needed to prevent drying. Transfer eggplant to large mixing bowl, stir to break up slices. Add tahini, garlic, extra virgin olive oil, lemon juice, crushed red pepper, salt and pepper to eggplant. Blend well. (Can also be done in food processor, using pulse motion to mix.) Garnish with parsley. Serve warm or chilled, with warm pita bread, lemon wedge, kalamata olives, sliced tomatoes and cucumbers.

Note: Grilling produces the best result, but eggplant can also be blackened over a gas flame for 5 to 10 minutes and baked in a 375-degree oven for 15 to 20 minutes, or simply baked whole for 30 to 40 minutes, until very soft. When done, scoop out flesh and chop coarsely.

Sauteed Shrimp and Vegetables and Feta Cheese
Tanyeri Grill

6 medium-large fresh mushrooms, cleaned and sliced
1 Tablespoon butter
1 small-medium green bell pepper, julienned
1 small-medium red bell pepper, julienned
1 small-medium yellow bell pepper, julienned
2 cloves garlic, minced
2 scallions, minced
1/4 cup feta cheese
1/2 teaspoon all-purpose flour
1/3 cup dry white wine
16 peeled and deveined large shrimp
1/2 teaspoon chopped fresh thyme or oregano
Pinch of dried tarragon
Pinch of paprika
Freshly ground black pepper, to taste

Saute mushrooms briefly in butter. Add peppers, garlic and scallions and saute over medium heat until vegetables are almost tender. Sprinkle flour over vegetables and add white wine, stirring quickly to avoid lumps. Lower heat. Stir in feta and shrimp, cover pan and simmer 3 to 4 minutes, until shrimp is cooked through. Add thyme (or oregano), tarragon, black pepper and paprika. Adjust seasonings to taste. (Note: Feta cheese is somewhat salty, so it is not necessary to add extra salt.) Portion shrimp and vegetables evenly onto warmed plates with rice pilaf on the side. Garnish with additional crumbled feta and chopped fresh parsley (optional).

Serves 2.

260

Joe A. Troia's
Basic Tomato Sauce

Described as a "chef and entrepreneur", the late Joe A. Troia's name rings a bell with everyone who knew him and enjoyed his culinary expertise. As a member of an early Greenbush Sicilian immigrant family, Troia merely carried on, with great love, the tradition of the food his mother prepared to serve to her family. The sauce recipe is from "Joe Troia's Specialties," a cookbook he compiled in 1983 to dedicate to his wife. The book was published two years later by his children, in his memory.

3 Tablespoons olive oil
1 1/2 cups chopped onion
3 cloves garlic, minced
1 (16-ounce) can plain tomatoes, crushed
1 (8-ounce) can tomato paste
3 1/2 cups water
1/2 teaspoon thyme
1/2 teaspoon basil
4 bay leaves
1 Tablespoon fresh chopped parsley
2 mint leaves, if available

Heat oil in heavy kettle and add onion and garlic, cook until tender. Add remaining ingredients and simmer for 1 hour, stirring often.

Note: Use as much of this recipe as you think necessary when making lasagna.

SUNNY SILVER PIE

Reflections of Otto's Inn, once located in Watertown, arrived from two readers after reader Joyce Deily shared her own remembrances of the 1940s when Otto's served sunny silver pie...

1/2 cup cold water
1 Tablespoon gelatin
4 egg yolks
3 Tablespoons lemon juice
Grated rind of 1 lemon
1 cup sugar
4 egg whites
Heavy cream, whipped
Baked pie shell

Set gelatin to soak in 1/2 cup water. Pour egg yolks, lemon juice, lemon rind and 1/2 cup sugar in a double boiler. Beat, while cooking, until creamy. When mixture gets thick, fold in the gelatin and beat well, allowing to cool. In another container, beat egg whites until light and quite stiff. Add 1/2 cup sugar, then fold into cooled custard. Pour into baked pie shell and chill in refrigerator for several hours. Serve with whipped cream.

Note: This makes a large pie.

Hoffman House Poppy Seed Torte

Sue Ellen Bergey remembers ordering this dessert each time she dined at the Hoffman House on East Washington Avenue where Aliota's is located today. Hoffman House President Dick Seal searched through his files and found the recipe, happy to have the opportunity to share it with Cooks' Exchange readers.

9x13-inch pan
6 cups milk
2 Tablespoons butter
1/2 cup corn starch (mix with milk)
1 teaspoon salt
1/2 cup of poppy seed
1 3/4 cups of sugar
2 teaspoons vanilla
8 egg yolks
Cook stirring constantly until mixture thickens.
BASE:
24 graham crackers
1/3 cup butter
Beat the 8 egg whites, gradually adding 1 cup of sugar until thick. Put the cracker mixture on the bottom of the pan. Add the thickened mixture to it, spreading evenly. Top with thickened egg whites and bake at 400 degrees for a few minutes or until topping turns brown.

My sister Elaine and me at
'Sunset Point' – Hoyt Park, Madison.

Celebrations

....•

FAITHFUL WEEKLY READERS OF MY WEEKLY
COLUMN IN THE WISCONSIN STATE JOURNAL KNOW
OF MY FONDNESS FOR HOYT PARK. Off Regent Street a
few blocks past West High School in an area of woods packed with
nostalgia, the park remains my favorite picnic spot and the
cherished location of wienie roasts held to celebrate my birthday
each Oct. 4 through my senior year of high school. Although
changes have taken place since then, the park is considered a
premier outdoor eating location by longtime Madisonians, as well
as those who discovered it as recently as yesterday.

A large stone shelter, carefully constructed by a hard-working
crew of immigrants, still stands as proud and tall as it did the day it
was completed some 50-odd years ago. And scattered throughout
the park are heavy stone fireplaces and matching tables waiting to
welcome picnickers, no matter what season. My love affair with
Hoyt Park began in the early 1940s when cooking outdoors was
done over wood fires made with dried twigs and old boards. Once
we arrived at the park and claimed "our" fireplace area by placing a
picnic basket on "our" table, Hoyt Park would become a world of
discoveries. Dressed in our autumn picnic attire of brown
gabardine jodhpurs and cardigan sweaters, my sister and I would
set out on our own. There were Indian trails to walk, and trails to
make from designs drawn with sticks in the dirt. Twigs were also
used to point hikers in different directions. The steep hill that
dropped away from our gathering spot could be negotiated with a
little practice and coordination. . . and by grabbing branches and
small trees on the way up or down. The expanse of the hill, which
today leads down to the dwellings on Bluff Street, were then
studded with the black raspberries I acquired an affinity for, as well

as sumac, with its maroon velvet fruit and leaves that became brilliant as fall set in. With wildflowers and brush skirting the way, the path in the ravine wound its way to the right and into an old stone quarry, which held abandoned equipment to tempt mischievous visitors. In the center of the quarry was a one-room concrete building, deserted and forever cool and damp in the heat of any warm day. With a window and door missing, the building had become shelter to crawly things, especially snakes that slithered under chunks of ceiling that had crumbled and dropped to the floor. There were countless other nooks and crannies in the park that we never tired of through the years, but we always set new goals to climb steeper hills or higher cliffs. When the smell of burning wood permeated the park and most of the nearby Sunset Village neighborhood, it was our signal that supper would soon be cooked and only then would another chapter of our young lives come to a close. Fresh-air appetites welcomed hot dogs, potato salad, chips, pickles, olives and birthday cake. And, somehow, there was always room left for marshmallows roasted over the finale of flickering flames.

Banana Cake

There were so many responses to a reader's request for banana cake that I wasn't sure which recipe to choose. When I read that Donna Wheadon's mother baked this cake in the 1940s for Donna's birthday, then shipped it from Cleveland to Syracuse just in time for the party, I decided that it must have been a very special favorite cake.

2 cups granulated sugar

1 cup shortening

2 eggs, beaten

6 medium bananas, mashed

3 cups unsifted all-purpose flour

2 teaspoons baking soda

1 teaspoon baking powder

Pinch of nutmeg

Pinch of salt

1 teaspoon vanilla

1 cup chopped nuts, floured with small amount from the 2 cups.

Cream sugar and shortening. Add eggs, then mashed bananas. Mix together dry ingredients and add to sugar mixture. Stir in vanilla and nuts tossed in flour. Bake in two greased and floured 9-inch cake pans and bake at 325 degrees for 50 minutes. Frost with favorite icing.

Caramel-Topped Applesauce Cake

This cake took first place at the New Albany, Indiana Harvest Baking Contest and was featured in Midwest Living magazine's "All-Time Best Recipe" cookbook. It was subsequently featured in my column Cooks' Exchange in response to Charlene Lauersdorg's request for eggless recipes to make for her granddaughter.

One (11-ounce) package raisins (2 cups)
Water
1 cup finely chopped black walnuts or pecans (8 ounces)
2 Tablespoons all-purpose flour
3/4 cup butter or margarine
2 cups sugar
2 cups applesauce
2 1/2 cups all-purpose flour
1 Tablespoon ground cinnamon
1 teaspoon baking soda
1 teaspoon ground nutmeg
Caramel Frosting

Place raisins in saucepan. Add enough water to cover. Bring to boiling. Remove from heat and let stand until cool. Drain off the water.

Toss nuts with 2 Tablespoons flour. Set aside. In mixing bowl beat butter or margarine for 30 seconds. Add sugar and beat until well combined. Beat in applesauce. In another bowl, combine the 2 1/2 cups flour with cinnamon, baking soda and nutmeg. Add to beaten mixture, beating until just combined. Stir in raisins and nuts. Turn batter into a greased and floured 10-inch pan. Bake in 350 degree oven for 65 to 70 minutes or until done. Cool in pan on rack for 20 minutes.

Remove from pan and let cool. Spoon Caramel Frosting over cake.

Makes 12 servings.

CARAMEL FROSTING:

In medium saucepan, heat 1/4 cup butter or margarine

and 1/2 cup packed brown sugar to boiling, stirring occasionally. Remove from heat. Stir in 2 tablespoons milk and 1 cup sifted powdered sugar. Beat with electric mixer until it becomes thick with a drizzling consistency.

Makes about 1 cup.

Burnt Sugar Cake

Former Madisonian Anita Pierce still faithfully reads the Wisconsin State Journal even though she resides way up in Boulder Junction. Shirley Schwoegler, Verona, responded to Pierce's request for an old fashioned burnt sugar cake.

To make caramelized sugar syrup: Place 1/2 cup sugar in skillet over medium heat and stir constantly until melted and quite dark. Remove from heat and add 1/4 cup hot water, stirring until dissolved. Cool.

CAKE:

3 cups cake flour
3 teaspoons baking powder
1/2 teaspoon salt
1/2 cup butter or margarine
1 1/2 cups sugar
3 egg yolks, well beaten
1 cup water
1 teaspoon vanilla
2 Tablespoons caramelized syrup
3 egg whites, stiffly beaten

Sift once and measure flour. Add baking powder and salt. Cream butter and gradually add sugar, creaming together until light and fluffy. Add well-beaten yolks and beat mixture thoroughly. Add flour mixture alternately with water, a small amount at a time. Beat after each addition until smooth. Add vanilla and caramelized syrup and blend. Fold in stiffly beaten egg whites. Bake in two greased 9-inch layer pans at 350 degrees for 25 to 30 minutes. Use a boiled icing with the remainder of caramelized syrup blended in.

BEST YET CHEESECAKE

Receiving compliments from readers fuels my enthusiasm each week. When Berwyn, Illinois, resident, Vincent Vertuno, contacted me it was with kind words and a cheesecake recipe made with cottage cheese as requested by a reader. Although the recipe was his all-time favorite dessert, he hadn't had the joy of a single slice for 14 years as the recipe had been misplaced. He searched for me, and for himself, until the recipe was finally found. Making it again merely reconfirmed what he already knew. It is the "best cheesecake. . . ever."

Crust: 2 cups graham cracker crumbs

1/3 cup brown sugar, packed

1/2 cup melted butter

1 teaspoon cinnamon

FILLING:

2 pounds Baker's cheese (or dry cottage cheese)

1 cup sugar

4 large eggs

2 Tablespoons fresh lemon juice

1 teaspoon vanilla

3 Tablespoons flour

One (14-ounce) can sweetened condensed milk (not evaporated)

Preheat oven to 350 degrees. Combine crust ingredients and press evenly across bottom and sides of 10-inch springform pan. Prepare filling by combining cheese and sugar and mixing well. Add eggs, one at a time, and mix well with each addition. Mix in lemon juice, vanilla and flour. Pour in condensed milk and mix until creamy, scraping sides of bowl as necessary. Pour all ingredients into prepared pan. Bake 60 minutes or until a knife inserted 1 inch from edge of pan comes out clean. Shut off oven and cool in oven with door open. Then refrigerate overnight. Cake will shrink from sides of pan. Can be topped with fruit topping or sour cream.

WINTERGREEN CAKE

With the inquisitiveness of someone, somewhere, a special cake was made by adding milk-soaked wintergreen candies. Wonders never cease.

38 pink wintergreen candies
1 1/4 cups milk
1/2 cup shortening
1 cup sugar
2 1/2 cups cake flour
2 teaspoons baking powder
1/4 teaspoon salt
4 egg whites, stiffly beaten

Soak wintergreen candies overnight in milk. The next day cream shortening and sugar. Combine dry ingredients. Add milk-candy mixture alternately with dry ingredients. Fold in egg whites. Bake in prepared layer pans for 25-35 minutes at 350 degrees. Frost with Fluffy White Frosting:

2 egg whites
3/4 cup white sugar
1/4 teaspoon cream of tartar
1/3 cup light corn syrup
2 Tablespoons water
1/4 teaspoon salt
1 teaspoon vanilla.

Combine all ingredients except vanilla in double boiler. Cook over boiling water, beating with electric mixer until mixture stands in peaks. Remove from heat and add vanilla.

Gum Drop Loaf Cake

Dian Gumpf has been making this cake for 20 years. She loves it for its flavor, its "jewel-like" appearance and the nostalgia it creates when reflecting back to when her daughter, Julie, then 1 1/2 years old, called it the "Dum Crock Cake"

1 cup butter or margarine

1 1/2 cups sugar

2 eggs

1 teaspoon vanilla

1 1/2 cups (15 1/2-ounce can) crushed pineapple, undrained

3 1/2 cups flour

1/2 teaspoon salt

1/2 teaspoon baking soda

1 teaspoon baking powder

1 cup golden raisins

1 cup sweetened, flaked coconut

1 cup pecans, broken

1 pound small gum drops, spice or fruit flavors (or cut up large ones)

Cream butter and sugar, then beat in eggs and vanilla. Add undrained pineapple. Mix or sift together dry ingredients, saving 2 Tablespoons to toss with raisins, coconut and nuts. Stir into batter. Add remaining ingredients with gum drops. Grease, flour and line bottoms of loaf pans with double layers of wax paper. Pour into prepared loaf pans and bake at 300 degrees for large, or 275 degrees for small pans for 1 to 1 1/2 hours. Allow to cool about 5 minutes in pans, then remove to racks and let cool thoroughly before slicing.

Yield: 2 large loaf pans or 3 small loaf pans

GRANNY'S CHOCOLATE MARVEL CAKE

Often made in New Glarus and Arlington, this cake contains only 1 gram of fat per two-layer serving, frosted.

2 cups all-purpose flour
1 cup unsweetened cocoa powder
2 cups granulated sugar
2 teaspoons baking soda
1 teaspoon baking powder
1/4 teaspoon salt
1 cup nonfat milk
Four 2 1/2-ounce jars baby-food pureed prunes
2 teaspoons vanilla extract
4 egg whites OR liquid egg substitute to equal 2 whole eggs
1 cup cappuccino (from mix) OR 2 teaspoons instant coffee in 1 cup boiling water OR 1 cup strong coffee
Nonstick cooking spray
4 cups Party Frosting (recipe follows)

Into large mixing bowl sift together flour, cocoa, sugar, baking soda, baking powder and salt. In medium bowl stir together milk, prunes, vanilla, egg whites or egg substitute and cappuccino or coffee. Pour moist ingredients into dry, blending well. Spray two 9-inch round baking pans with nonstick spray. Divide batter equally between pans. Bake in preheated 350 degree oven 30 to 35 minutes or until center tests done with wooden pick. Let cakes cool in pans 10 minutes. Invert onto wire rack; cool. Frost with Party Frosting.

PARTY FROSTING:

1 1/2 cups light brown sugar, packed
3 egg whites
1/4 cup cappuccino OR 1 tablespoon instant coffee in 1/4 cup boiling water OR 1/4 cup strong coffee
1 teaspoon cream of tartar
1 teaspoon vanilla extract

In bottom of large double boiler, bring water to boil then reduce to simmer. In top, combine brown sugar, egg

274

whites, cappuccino or coffee and cream of tartar. Beat with mixer 5 to 7 minutes or until stiff peaks form. Remove from heat. Add vanilla and beat additional 3 minutes.

Note: This cake tastes rich enough to be served without frosting. Simply dust top with powdered sugar.

HICKORY NUT CAKE

This is the first cake recipe to appear in my Wednesday column in the Wisconsin State Journal. As a favorite of Joan Johnson, Columbus, also attached was her favorite marshmallow frosting.

   1/2 cup butter or shortening
   1 1/2 cups white sugar
   1 teaspoon vanilla
   2 cups sifted cake flour
   2 teaspoons baking powder
   1/4 teaspoon salt
   3/4 cup milk
   4 egg whites, stiffly beaten
   1 cup finely chopped hickory nuts
   Mock marshmallow frosting (recipe follows)

Cream butter, sugar and vanilla together until fluffy. Sift flour, baking powder and salt together and add alternately with milk to creamed mixture. Beat until smooth. Fold in nuts and egg whites.

Pour into 9x13-inch greased pan. Bake at 350 degrees for 25 to 30 minutes.

Note: For best flavor, cover this cake and let stand a day before serving

MOCK MARSHMALLOW FROSTING

2 1/2 Tablespoons flour
1/2 cup milk
1/2 cup sugar
1/2 cup softened butter or margarine
1/2 teaspoon vanilla
1/2 cup chopped hickory nuts, optional

Place flour in small saucepan. Add milk gradually, stirring constantly until mixture is smooth and blended. Place mixture over moderately low heat and cook, stirring constantly, until thickened and smooth. Mixture will be fairly stiff. Cool. Place butter in small bowl of an electric mixer and beat until creamy. Add sugar gradually and beat until mixture is light. Add the cooled flour mixture and beat at high speed until light and fluffy, about 1 or 2 minutes. Gently fold in vanilla and mix in about 1/2 cup chopped hickory nuts (optional) before frosting cake.

Blue Ribbon Pound Cake

Submitted by Joan Howe for the 1985 Wisconsin State Journal cookbook, this delicious vanilla-flavored creation captured first place honors in the Cakes and Tortes category.

2 cups butter

3 cups sugar

6 eggs

1 1/2 teaspoons vanilla

4 cups sifted cake flour

2/3 cup milk

Powdered sugar

Cream together butter and sugar until light and fluffy. Add eggs, one at a time, beating well after each addition. Add vanilla. Total beating time should be 10 minutes. Add flour alternately with milk, beating well after each addition. Pour batter into a well-greased 10-inch fluted tube pan. Bake at 350 degrees for 1 1/4 hours or until cake tests done. Cool in pan or rack for 15 minutes. Remove from pan; cool on rack. Dust with powdered sugar. Cake is best if covered and allowed to stand 24 hours before serving.

Yield: 12 servings.

"Real" Marshmallow Frosting

1 cup sugar
1/2 cup boiling water
1/4 teaspoon vinegar
2 egg whites, stiffly beaten
10 marshmallows, cut in small pieces

Combine sugar, boiling water and vinegar in a saucepan and stir over heat until sugar is dissolved. Cover for 2 minutes to prevent crystals forming and cook without stirring. Remove cover and cook until candy thermometer registers 238 degrees or until a small amount dropped into a cup of cold water forms a soft ball. Pour in a thin stream over stiffly beaten egg whites, beating constantly. Add marshmallow pieces and continue beating until cool and thick enough to spread.

WALDORF ASTORIA CAKE

It has been referred to as Rose Cake, Red Velvet Cake, Christmas Cake and Valentine Cake, but made its first appearance as the Waldorf Astoria Cake as the result, no doubt, of a creative chef in the hotel kitchen.

1/2 cup Crisco
1 1/2 cups sugar
2 eggs
2 ounces red food coloring
1 teaspoon vanilla
1 Tablespoon cocoa
1 teaspoon salt
1 cup buttermilk
2 1/4 cups cake flour
1 teaspoon baking soda
1 teaspoon vinegar
FROSTING:
3 Tablespoons flour
1 cup milk
1 cup sugar
1 cup margarine
1 teaspoon vanilla

Preheat oven to 350 degrees. Mix together vinegar and baking soda; set aside. Cream sugar, Crisco and eggs. Make paste of coloring and cocoa and add to sugar mixture. Add buttermilk and salt alternately with flour. Add vanilla, and lastly, fold in baking soda-vinegar mixture. Bake in three 9-inch greased, floured pans for 30 minutes. Cool.

FROSTING:

Cook flour and milk until thick. Cool. Cream sugar, margarine and vanilla. Beat together 5 minutes. Frost cake.

Note: This cake should be stored in the refrigerator.

Favortie Frostings

FLUFFY WHITE FROSTING:

1 box powdered sugar, sifted

Dash of salt

2 unbeaten egg whites

1 stick margarine

1/2 cup shortening

2 teaspoons vanilla

Yellow food coloring

Beat all ingredients with a few drops of food coloring for a fairly long time to increase volume and make fluffy. Freeze any leftover.

CARAMEL FROSTING:

3 cups brown sugar

1/2 cup milk or cream

4 Tablespoons butter

2 Tablespoons vanilla

Bring to boil and boil for 3 minutes, stirring constantly. Remove from heat. Beat until creamy, adding a little more milk or cream, if necessary for easier spreading. This will make enough for top and sides of 9x13-inch cake.

BANANA FROSTING:

1/2 cup mashed ripe banana

1/2 teaspoon lemon juice

4 Tablespoons butter

3 cups powdered sugar, or enough for desired consistency

Mix banana and lemon juice. Cream butter. Add approximately 3 cups of powdered sugar alternately with the banana mixture to the creamed butter.

Emblem on a wall at Breese Stevens
Field on East Washington Avenue.

Tasty nostalgia

· ·

CHILLY EVENING TEMPERATURES AND CHEERS FROM WARNER PARK TELL ME THAT CITY HIGH SCHOOL FOOTBALL SEASON HAS BEGUN, AND MY MIND AUTOMATICALLY SCOOTS BACK TO THE 1950S AND BREESE STEVENS FIELD ON EAST WASHINGTON AVENUE. I was a student at East then, and the stadium was within walking distance for many of us. Best friends would gather after summer to walk the center of the grassy boulevard on the avenue and follow the glow of stadium lights like a brilliant star leading the way. A nickel would pay for a quick bus ride, but walking was much more fun.

East, Central and West played their games there on Friday and Saturday nights, while Edgewood and Wisconsin High occupied the stadium during the afternoon. Although many other sporting events took place at Breese Stevens, I remember best the football games where the local and conference greats ran, threw, kicked, blocked and tackled. When the games ended, we'd start another trek, this time toward Downtown and East Doty Street, to a place called the LOFT. Built in 1925, the field was named for Breese J. Stevens, former Madison mayor and civic leader. East and Central had been playing their games at Camp Randall but exited the college campus when the new stadium for high school competition was completed. Initially an open field with a chain-link fence, a thick wall with rock quarried from Hoyt Park was built between 1934 and 1940 as a Civil Works Administration project, thus providing protection for the surrounding streets and homes. That stadium became a powerful entity in the lives of decades of high school students and sports enthusiasts alike. And when suggestion was made in the early 1980s by city parks officials to have the grand

- old stone landmark demolished, hearts sank. Public outcry created some quick soul-searching at City Hall and, because of protests from a meaningful cross-section of Madison, Breese Stevens Field remains more than just a memory for all who passed through its iron gates with a ticket in hand. I'm glad it's still there. I'll never understand why yesterday seems to have deadlines that cause joys of the past to disappear. And, of course, it becomes even more important to preserve structures when sentimental attachments are involved. Breese Stevens is where my father tucked the pigskin under his arm in the 1920s and dazzled the city with his "flashy" halfback maneuvers for Coach Howie Johnson and the red-brick Downtown high school called Central. It is also where I performed on chilly autumn evenings in my heavy purple-and-gold cheerleader sweater to witness and savor with good friends what being a Madison teen-ager was like– 40 years ago. Recipes have sentimental attachments, too, especially the good-tasting ones prepared and served when the economy and world situations didn't allow a daily feast on every table in every neighborhood. It was back when extra sugar was hidden in closets and attics and fingers were crossed that authorities wouldn't learn of such forbidden treasures.

Peanut Brittle

Mauston resident, Frances McNown, 83, found this "no-fail" recipe in a 1948 UW Extension bulletin in answer to a request of Baraboo resident Mary Haugsby.

2 cups sugar
1/2 cup white corn syrup
1 cup water
3 cups salted peanuts
1 teaspoon butter
1/4 teaspoon baking soda

Mix sugar, syrup and water in a kettle. Boil until the syrup forms a soft ball in cold water. Put peanuts in a wire strainer and shake off excess salt. Add peanuts to the syrup and cook until syrup is a golden brown. Stir occasionally. Add butter and baking soda. Pour on a large greased tray or cookie sheet. Stretch out thin with buttered fingers just before it hardens. When cold, break into pieces.

DUMPLINGS

• "light-as-a-feather" dumplings from Mary Jane Anderson.

1 cup flour
1/4 teaspoon salt
2 teaspoons baking powder
1 egg
Milk

Use enough milk to make a stiff dough. Drop by spoonfuls into hot broth containing deboned, skinless chicken.

Cook on medium burner for 10 minutes, covered, then an additional 10 minutes, uncovered. (She states that this is the opposite of what cookbooks instruct one to do and insists they are wrong.)

Note: Another suggestion is to prepare dumpling dough, then let it stand for at least 30 minutes before lowering spoonfuls into the broth. This helps to make dumplings extra fluffy.

German Prune-Apple Dressing

When Faye Underdahl was a little girl, her mother would send her to the basement fruit and vegetable cellar during the holidays for "greeny" apples and an onion, "the size of a quarter" to use in the stuffing of a goose or duck. That was 60 years ago and although the amount of the onion remains the same, the "greenies" have been replaced with Granny Smith apples.

One 12-ounce box or package of dried pitted prunes
4 cups dried bread cubes
2 Granny Smith apples, cored, but not peeled, chopped quite fine
1 onion the size of a quarter, chopped very fine
1 Tablespoon sugar
1 teaspoon salt
1 teaspoon cloves, or according to taste

Put prunes in saucepan, cover with water. Bring to boil, turn off heat and cover with sauce pan. Let stand for at least an hour. Mix all ingredients together. If bread is not really moist, add water until it becomes the desired consistency. Additional apples and bread can be used, if needed or wanted.

Baked Prune Pudding

In 1935, Ida Bailey wrote The Service Cookbook exclusively for the F.W. Woolworth Company. Years later it has become a return visit and reminder to the past and our beloved "dime" stores.

2 cups whole wheat bread crumbs
1/2 cup milk
1/4 cup prune juice
Juice of 1/2 orange
2 eggs, beaten
1 Tablespoon melted butter or margarine
3/4 cup granulated sugar
1 cup chopped prunes
Cream or jelly sauce (recipe below)

Mix crumbs with milk and prune and orange juice, the eggs and butter; add sugar and prunes. Stir well. Transfer to a greased dish and bake 30 minutes at 350 degrees. Serve with cream or jelly sauce.

JELLY SAUCE:
4 ounces tart jelly, any flavor
1/2 cup boiling water
1 Tablespoon butter or margarine
1 Tablespoon flour

Combine jelly with boiling water. Boil until jelly is melted and thickened with flour and butter creamed together. Stir and cook until smooth and thick.

Great-Uncle Walter's Slumgullion

Four months into my column, I sensed the education I was getting with recipes of food I had never heard of. When a postcard arrived with a request for slumgullion, I had to turn to my "Cook's Dictionary" to make certain it was being spelled correctly. Many readers responded, each with a nostalgic recollection of the slumgullion served in their house. From World War I and the army camps in France, to the wilderness of California and Alaska, slumgullion seemed to satisfy the taster with a variety of appearances and flavors, depending on where it was prepared and served. This recipe was a favorite of Karen Muse's great-uncle Walter, a lifelong bachelor with a unique personality and a love of the outdoors.

1 1/2 cups dry macaroni
1 pound ground beef, browned and drained
1 cup chopped onion
2 garlic cloves, chopped
1/2 cup chopped green pepper
2 8-ounce cans tomato sauce
One 16-ounce can whole kernel corn, undrained
Salt to taste
1 teaspoon chili powder
1/2 teaspoon sugar
1 1/2 cups cubed sharp Cheddar cheese

Boil macaroni for amount of time directed on package.

Brown ground beef with onion, garlic and green pepper. Drain well. Add tomato sauce, corn and spices to drained meat-and-vegetable mixture. In a 2 1/2-quart dish, layer half of cooked macaroni, then half of meat mixture, then half of cheese. Repeat. Bake, uncovered, at 350 degrees for approximately 40 minutes.

MAINE SLUMGULLION

Clipped by Holly Bashford from the Maine Sunday Telegram in 1973 and the Cooking Down East food column by Marjorie Standish, this has all the ingredients of what we today call. . . comfort food.

2 pounds of stew beef
4 onions
1 large can tomatoes,(1 quart if home canned)
1 teaspoon poultry seasoning
Salt to taste
1/3 cup flour
1/2 cup cold water

Cut stew beef into 1-inch cubes. Do not brown. Place in a 2-quart casserole pan. Cover with sliced onions. Salt the onions. Turn canned tomatoes over onions, add another sprinkle of salt and 1 teaspoon poultry seasoning. Cover pan; use foil if no cover is available. Bake at 275 to 300 degrees for three hours. In meantime, combine 1/3 cup flour and 1/2 cup cold water; mix and allow to stand, as this prevents lumping when stirred into hot beef mixture. When meat is tender, stir in the flour mixture; this thickens the slumgullion immediately.

Serves 6 to 8.

Note: This dish freezes well. Serve with mashed potatoes or on cooked noodles.

1918 Nut Hash

"Forgotten Recipes" will tug at your heartstrings. Published by the Country Store in Greendale, Wis., the cookbook exudes nostalgia on each page, stirring memories of the past, no matter how old or young you happen to be.

2 Tablespoons bacon drippings
2 Tablespoons minced onion
2 Tablespoons peanut butter
1 cup milk
1 quart chopped cooked potatoes
1 cup chopped celery
1 cup broken nut meats
1 shredded green pepper
Salt and pepper to taste

Put drippings in frying pan. Add minced onion and fry until it is a deep yellow. Add peanut butter and milk next, stirring constantly until everything comes to a boil. Add potatoes, celery, nut meats and green pepper and season with salt and pepper. Mix thoroughly. Cook for about 30 minutes over a low flame and stir occasionally. Serve hot.

PRESIDENT'S SORGHUM CAKE

As one of the first Wisconsin State Journal readers to write a letter to my column, Cooks' Exchange, Lela Jacobson described the sorghum crops of the past, and how it was gathered and boiled, then used as a substitute for molasses and sugar. She wondered if I could supply her with a recipe for sorghum cake. I located this in "The Presidents' Cookbook, written by Poppy Cannon and Patricia Brooks," and used it even though it calls for both sorghum and sugar.

1/2 cup butter
1 cup sugar
1 egg, slightly beaten
1 cup sorghum syrup
2 cups sifted flour
1/4 teaspoon nutmeg
1/4 teaspoon cinnamon
1 teaspoon soda
1 teaspoon baking powder
1 cup sour milk

Cream together butter and sugar, slowly adding lightly beaten egg and sorghum syrup. Beat well. Add alternately to mixture dry ingredients and sour milk. When all are added, beat well again. Bake in greased and floured loaf pan in 325-degree oven for 1 hour or until done. Cake may be frosted with any favorite frosting

Note: Loaf pan size is undetermined.

BROWNSTONE FRONT
CHOCOLATE CAKE

Loyal reader Pam Valenta went searching for Lela Jacobson's request for the Brownstone Front Chocolate Cake and found the recipe the "New Cook Book" published in 1933 by the Jewel Tea Company.

2/3 cup butter

1 1/2 cups sugar

3 eggs, separated

1 teaspoon baking soda

1 cup milk

2 cups sifted pastry flour

3/4 cup cocoa

1/2 teaspoon salt

1/2 teaspoon vanilla

Cream butter; add sugar and cream well. Beat yolks. Dissolve baking soda in milk and add alternately with sifted dry ingredients. Add vanilla. Beat egg whites stiff and fold into batter. Bake in three prepared layer pans in a 375 degree oven for 25 to 30 minutes. Cool and remove.

Note: Valenta suggests sifting flour two or three times before the final measurement of 2 cups is made if you plan to use all-purpose flour.

AUNT TILLY'S
COTTAGE CHEESE CAKE

Treasured by Marva Manthe's family, this cheesecake recipe was "inherited" 50 years ago and named for great-aunt Otilia Wheeler of rural Brodhead.

CRUST:

1/2 cup cake flour

1 teaspoon baking powder

1/4 teaspoon salt

1/2 cup sugar

1/2 cup butter

1 egg, slightly beaten

Combine all ingredients like pie crust, using egg for liquid. Line a 5-inch-deep torte pan.

FILLING

1 1/2 pounds cottage cheese

1 1/2 cups sugar

5 egg yolks

2 Tablespoons melted butter

Juice and grated rind of one lemon

1/4 cup cake flour

1/4 teaspoon nutmeg

5 egg whites

2 Tablespoons cream

Sieve cottage cheese twice (or blend in blender until smooth). Add sugar, egg yolks, melted butter, lemon juice and rind, flour and nutmeg. Fold in stiffly beaten egg whites and cream. Pour into crust. Bake at 425 degrees for five minutes, reduce heat to 325 degrees and bake until filling is firm, about 45 to 60 minutes.

War Cake

"Thrifty Recipes for Thrifty Housewives" was found in Pam Valenta's vast cookbook collection. Proceeds from this fundraising book went to the Red Cross.

2/3 cup shortening
2 cups brown sugar
2 cups water
4 cups flour, sifted
2 teaspoons baking powder
1 cup raisins
1 teaspoon cinnamon
1 teaspoon allspice
1/2 teaspoon nutmeg
1/2 teaspoon cloves
1 teaspoon salt
1/2 teaspoon baking soda
1 Tablespoon hot water
1/2 cup chopped nuts

Boil shortening, brown sugar, water and spices for three minutes. Pour into a large bowl and cool to lukewarm. Mix flour and baking powder and add with nuts. Beat well. Add soda mixed with 1 Tablespoon of water. Pour into a greased loaf pan and bake for 30 to 40 minutes in a 350 degree oven.

Note: dried apples, apricots, prunes or figs can be substituted for raisins.

The apple tree after an early snowstorm.

The old apple tree

.... •

APPLE PIE FOR BREAKFAST? MY MOTHER WILL
SMILE WHEN SHE READS THIS. SHE KNOWS IT'S
TRUE. I was the one who would get up before anyone else on
Sunday mornings, slice a piece of leftover pie, then sprawl out on
the floor with the newspaper and the funnies. Actually, it didn't
have to be apple pie. Any kind would do. Rhubarb in spring, peach
in the summer, apple and pumpkin during fall, cherry for George
Washington's birthday in February and pizza throughout the year.
Pie was pie, but it was especially good with the apples from our
tree.

When we moved into our house in 1941, there was a snow apple
tree in the back yard that produced apples with a pure snowy white
flesh. The first year there greeted us with a spring of splendid pink
and white blossoms complemented by purple violets that
surrounded the tree like a soft blanket. The tree was destined to
become my good friend. An old, heavy arm held my swing, and its
other branches supported me a few years later when I'd climb high
with my $2.14 Brownie camera . . . and a salt shaker stuck deep in
my bluejeans pocket. I loved sitting way up where the robins and
squirrels rested, but the real fun would start in August when little
green apples began to fill out. Perfect for an antsy kid, a shake of
salt, and two tiny bites . . . each. No one could convince me that
apples like that were awful tasting. I had a mind of my own and
thought it was an experience I deserved. The great thing about it
was that I never got sick from the sour little things. Green apple
tasting time became an annual affair until I turned 16 and much
wiser.

Apple Syrup

- 12 pounds ripe, juicy cooking apples

Wash apples and drain well. Cut up roughly, but do not peel or core. Start with about 2/3 of the apples. Put this amount into large pan and barely cover with water. Bring to boil and cook until fruit is partially broken down. Drain liquid into second pan and add rest of apples, cut up. Return to boil and simmer, covered, for one hour. Strain through a jelly bag overnight. Apple butter can be made from leftover solids. Measure juice and have ready to add: 1/2 pound (2 1/4 cups) sugar for each 2 1/2 cups apple juice; 4 whole cloves, optional; 2-inch stick of cinnamon. Boil juice 15 minutes in large pan. Remove from heat and add sugar and spices. Stir to dissolve sugar. Return to boil and boil gently for 30 minutes. Skim off any foam, remove spices and seal in sterile jars. A drop of red food color may add eye appeal.

Yield: 5 pints.

Apple Spice Syrup

You have no idea how difficult it was to secure an apple syrup recipe from orchard owners. Many claimed no knowledge of such a recipe, while others were obvious with their protection of them. Five readers came through for me with one from Taste of Home a wonderful magazine of recipes from the great cooks of America, and another from Gladys Mann's "Home Preserving and Bottling."

1/4 cup packed brown sugar

2 Tablespoons cornstarch

1/4 teaspoon ground allspice

1/8 teaspoon ground nutmeg

1 3/4 cups apple juice or cider

In a saucepan, combine brown sugar, cornstarch, allspice and nutmeg and mix well. Add juice or cider. Cook and stir over medium heat until syrup is bubbling and slightly thickened. Serve with apple pancakes. Makes 1 3/4 cups. From a recent issue of the "Taste of Home" magazine.

Oven Apple Butter

Found in the reliable "Farm Journal Country Cookbook," apple butter made in the oven sounded like it might be exactly what Lola Whitney requested in time for the fall apple harvest.

2 quarts water
2 Tablespoons salt
6 pounds apples, cored, peeled and sliced
2 quarts sweet cider
3 1/2 to 4 cups sugar
1 teaspoon ground cinnamon
1/2 teaspoon ground cloves
1/2 teaspoon ground allspice

Combine water and salt. Add apples. Drain well but do not rinse slices. Put through food chopper, using finest blade. Measure pulp and juice (there should be 2 quarts). Combine with cider. Place in large enamel pan. Center pan in moderate oven (350 degree). Let simmer 3 to 3 1/2 hours until cooked down about half and mixture is thick and mushy. Stir thoroughly every half hour. Put mixture through sieve or food mill; it should yield 2 1/4 to 2 1/2 quarts. Combine sugar and spices; add to sauce and return to oven. Continue simmering about 1 1/2 hours or until thick, stirring every half hour. To test, pour small amount onto cold plate. If no liquid oozes around edge, apple butter is cooked. Pour into hot jars; adjust lids and process in boiling water bath (212 degrees) 10 minutes. Remove jars and complete seals unless closures are self-sealing kind.

Makes 2 quarts.

APPLE CRISP PIE

One of my own favorites, discovered a few years ago in a Williams-Sonoma catalog.

Single pastry crust for a 9-inch pie dish
3 to 4 large pie apples
2 Tablespoons sugar
3/4 cup sugar
3/4 cup flour
1/2 teaspoon cinnamon
1/4 teaspoon salt
8 Tablespoons chilled, cubed, unsalted butter

Peel, core and slice apples. Toss with 2 tablespoons sugar. Fill pastry shell, rounding up in center. Combine 3/4 cup sugar, flour, cinnamon and salt. Mix in butter with fingertips or pastry blender until granular; sprinkle evenly over apples. Bake for 15 minutes in 425 degree oven. Reduce heat to 350 degrees and bake another 30 minutes until golden brown. Serve warm with vanilla ice cream.

MOM'S APPLE PIE

The description of a pie remembered from the 1960s included being partially baked, then pouring cream through the slits of the crust before returning it to the oven to complete the baking process. Nancy Annen, Madison; Doris Hendrickson, Monroe; and Janice Geotz, Lodi are responsible for submitting this recipe.

1 basic pie crust
1 cup sugar
2 Tablespoons all-purpose flour
2 generous teaspoons ground cinnamon
3/4 teaspoon ground nutmeg
3 1/2 cups peeled, cored and sliced McIntosh apples (about 4 to 5 apples)
3 cups peeled, cored and sliced Granny Smith apples (about 4 apples)
2 Tablespoons lightly salted butter
1/2 cup heavy or whipping cream

Prepare pie crust and divide it into two equal portions. On lightly floured surface, roll out half the dough to a thickness of 1/8 inch. Ease it gently into a 9-inch pie pan; trim the overhang to 3/4 inch. Set it aside. Roll out the remaining dough to thickness of 1/16 inch and set it aside. Preheat oven to 400 degrees. Combine sugar, flour and spices in large bowl. Add apple slices and toss until they are well coated. Fill crust with apple slices and dot with butter. Ease top crust over filled bottom crust, trim the overhang to 3/4 inch. Fold top crust over bottom. Crimp to seal edges. Cut slits in top crust to allow steam to escape. Bake for 1 hour or until crust is golden and apples test done. Turn off oven and remove pie. Gently pour cream through slits in crust. Return pie to oven and leave it there until oven is nearly cool, about 20 minutes. Serve immediately.

Note: To prevent crust edges from overbrowning, tear circle from a sheet of aluminum foil and place sheet loosely over pie, leaving center of crust exposed.

302

Apple Doughnuts

Deep fried apple doughnuts created a little extra searching for Sharon Damrow of Marshall. The orchard grower in Bayfield County who makes and sells what Damrow remembers, wouldn't part with her recipe. In the meantime, Kathleen Moe, Sun Prairie, who refers to these as doughnuts, gives us a recipe to suffice while the search continues.

3 cups flour
1/8 teaspoon salt
1 teaspoon nutmeg
4 teaspoons baking powder
1 cup sugar
2/3 cup shortening
2 eggs, beaten
1/2 cup milk
1 cup grated apples
TOPPING:
Melted butter
1 cup sugar
2 Tablespoons cinnamon

Combine all dry ingredients. Cut in shortening; add eggs, milk and grated apples. Stir just enough to mix. Spoon into either large or small muffin tins, half full. Bake at 350 degrees for 20-25 minutes. Remove from pan while hot. Dip in melted butter, then in mixture of 1 cup sugar and 2 Tablespoons cinnamon.

APPLE DOUGHUTS II

A deep fried apple doughnut recipe finally surfaced from Shirley Munson and Jo Nelson's "Apple Lovers Cookbook."

1 package active dry yeast
1/2 teaspoon sugar
3/4 cup warm milk
2 cups flour
2 Tablespoons sugar
1/8 teaspoon salt
2 eggs, beaten
1/2 cup raisins
1/2 cup peeled, diced apples
3 Tablespoons diced or minced mixed candied fruit
1 teaspoon grated lemon peel
Cooking oil
Confectioners' sugar

Sprinkle yeast and 1/2 teaspoon sugar on milk; stir to dissolve. Let stand 10 minutes. Sift together flour, 2 Tablespoons sugar and salt into bowl. Make a well in the center. Add yeast and eggs; mix just until blended. Stir in raisins, apples, candied fruit and lemon peel. Cover and let rise in warm place until doubled, about one hour. Drop batter by heaping Tablespoonfuls into deep hot oil (360 degrees), frying until golden brown, about three minutes. Drain on paper towels. Dust with confectioners' sugar.

Makes 15.

Note: Doughnuts should be sugared just before serving by shaking one at a time in a paper bag with granulated or powdered sugar or a mixture of sugar and cinnamon. Doughnuts can also be served with hot applesauce topped with whipped cream or ice cream.

APPLE CUSTARD KUCHEN

Arelene Radloff, Waterloo, requested a recipe for apple kuchen with puddles of cream on top. Inez Bachman, Blue Mounds, responded with her mother-in-law's favorite kuchen recipe.

2 cups flour
1/4 teaspoon baking powder
Pinch of salt
1/2 cup sugar
1/2 cup butter
8 to 10 apples
1/2 cup sugar
Cinnamon, to taste
3 eggs, beaten
1 1/2 cups cream or Carnation evaporated milk

Mix flour, baking powder, salt and sugar together and cut in butter until mixture is crumbly and the size of peas. Save 3/4 cup for later. Pat remaining mixture in a 12x18-inch ungreased pan. Peel, core and slice apples, arranging them over crust by overlapping slices. Mix the reserved crumbs with an additional 1/2 cup sugar and cinnamon. Sprinkle over apples. Bake at 350 degrees for 20 minutes. Remove from oven. Carefully pour mixture of eggs and cream over the top and bake an additional 25 minutes.

Note: This is also delicious with fresh peaches.

Apple Pecan Pancakes

". . . from the recipe collection of Maggie Lomasney."

1 cup flour
2 Tablespoons brown sugar
2 teaspoons baking powder
1/2 teaspoon salt
1/2 teaspoon ground cinnamon
3/4 cup plus; 2 Tablespoons milk
2 eggs, separated
1 teaspoon vanilla
1/2 cup finely chopped, peeled apple
1/2 cup finely chopped pecans

In a bowl, combine flour, brown sugar, salt and cinnamon. Stir in milk, egg yolks and vanilla. Add apples and pecans. Beat egg whites until stiff peaks form. Fold into batter. Use 1/4 cup each and pour into hot skillet. Turn when bubbles form and break, and edge of pancake is golden brown. Cook second side until golden brown.

Yield: 12 pancakes

Danish Pastry Apple Bars

When Jean Carlson called me about an apple square recipe that appeared about 20 years ago in the Wisconsin State Journal, I was certain she meant the recipe Mary Borenz shared with staff member Ann Rundell for an article she was writing.

3 cups flour
1 teaspoon salt
1 cup margarine or butter
1 egg, separated
Milk (see amount in instructions)
1 cup corn flakes
10-12 apples, peeled, cored and sliced
1 cup sugar
1 teaspoon cinnamon
1 cup powdered sugar, sifted
1/4 cup milk

Combine flour and salt; cut in margarine or butter. Separate egg, saving white. Beat yolk and add enough milk to make 2/3 cup liquid: stir into flour mixture. Roll half the dough to 17x12 inches and fit into large (10x15-inch) jellyroll pan. Sprinkle with corn flakes and top with apples. Combine sugar and cinnamon; sprinkle over apples. Roll remaining dough and place over apples. Beat egg white until frothy; brush on crust. Bake at 375 degrees for 50 minutes. Combine sifted powdered sugar with 1/4 cup milk and drizzle over warm bars.

APPLE BREAD

A request for an apple bread recipe brought in a cache of favorites, each described as delicious. A final decision was difficult. Since Lucy Faherty, Platteville, served her apple bread as a dessert and Wheaton, Ill., school principal Edith Leur, is known for her sweet breads as well as for never giving out her recipes.

4 cups chopped apples
1 cup salad oil
2 eggs, beaten
2 cups sugar
2 1/2 cups flour
1 teaspoon cinnamon
1 teaspoon baking soda
1/2 teaspoon salt
1 teaspoon vanilla

Mix apples, oil, eggs and sugar. Let stand 20 minutes. Add remaining ingredients. Mix well. Pour into two greased and floured 8 1/2x4 1/2x2 1/2-inch loaf pans. Bake about 1 hour at 350 degrees or until bread tests done. Cool slightly and remove from pans. Freezes well.

Yield: 2 loaves.

Grandpa Joe Kovacs, me and Rusty.

Thanksgiving

. . . .•

"Bless us, O Lord, and these thy gifts". . .
was the beginning of the prayer my family
said before each meal. One of the "gifts" for
Thanksgiving Day in 1944 happened to be "Rusty," my pet Rock
Cornish rooster. No one seems to remember where Rusty came
from since every visit to a farm as a child found me returning home
with a tiny creature on my lap. Carefully heeding the advice of
every farmer never seemed to be enough for me to be a surrogate
mother, as each baby chick I adopted went to heaven within a week
or two. For whatever reason, Rusty survived the summer and ended
up gracing an oval platter late in November. I had had my share of
dogs and cats, but owning a rooster was magnificent. Rusty, with
his dark, shiny, rust-colored feathers, made me the happiest kid in
the neighborhood. During the day, with a string tied loosely
around his neck, Rusty strutted under the apple tree, around the
bridal wreath, and through the gardens like he was king of a
farmyard. The only difference was that the ground underfoot was
soft green city grass and, instead of a barn to sleep in, he retired
each night within the confines of our small screened-in back porch.
My Hungarian-born Grandpa liked the rooster as much as me. He
and I would sit together on a bench, while Grandpa smoked either
his pipe or cigar and talked to Rusty in broken English between
puffs. Meanwhile, I would be hugging, petting and conversing with
a rooster whose jerky motions and head tilting made me believe
that my pet understood everything I said. It made getting up each
morning more fun than before, and going to bed at night with a
smile knowing Rusty had a cozy cardboard box to sleep in. When
November arrived and Rusty approached a good feast weight of
about 6 to 8 pounds, he became the topic of more than one after-

hours discussion in ways I would never have wanted to eavesdrop on. There was no kind way of breaking the news to me that my pet rooster would soon strut one last time before becoming headless and featherless and popped into a hot oven to roast. My tears were not convincing. It was time, they said. No smiles broke my pout at the table that Thanksgiving Day as I sat before a platter heaped with the pet I had loved and cared for. Actually, I think everyone felt a little guilty about the "gift" that was being served, except for my sister, who, as usual, was more concerned about the number of peas she could hide under her mashed potatoes. Had it not been for an additional turkey prepared that day, my seventh Thanksgiving feast would have been as a vegetarian.

APPLE CIDER RAISIN STUFFING

Joan Fiedler has prepared this cider stuffing in her Middleton home every Thanksgiving since 1960.

16 to 20 slices of bread that have been cubed (about a 1 1/2pound loaf of bread)

4 medium sized apples (about 4 cups diced), which have been pared, cored, quartered and diced

2/3 cup chopped celery with leaves

1/3 to 2/3 cup chopped onion

1 1/2 cups raisins

3/4 to 1 1/4 cups melted butter or margarine

3 teaspoons salt

1 1/2 teaspoons Accent

2 teaspoons marjoram

1/2 teaspoon pepper

3/4 to 1 1/4 cups sweet apple cider

Lay bread slices out on counter the night before so bread will be slightly dry rather than too soft. Cube bread and add apples, celery, onion and raisins. In another bowl, mix together melted butter with seasonings. Pour over bread mixture. Add apple cider, tossing lightly until mixed. Spoon stuffing lightly into neck and body cavities of turkey. Do not pack. This will stuff a 15-pound turkey. Place extra stuffing in baking dish and bake, covered with the turkey, the last hour of baking time. Leftovers freeze well.

CROCK POT DRESSING

•   Mary Lou Haskins, Lancaster, prepares this crock pot-slow cooker poultry dressing because it is moist, has seasonings that are easily adjusted, and frees needed space in her Thanksgiving oven.

1 cup butter or margarine, melted
2 cups chopped onion
2 cups chopped celery
1/4 cup parsley (fresh or dried)
2 cups canned mushrooms, drained
2 eggs, beaten
3 1/2 to 4 1/2 cups chicken broth, or enough to moisten well
13 cups cubed dry bread
1 1/2 teaspoon poultry seasoning
2 teaspoons salt
2 teaspoons sage
1 teaspoon thyme
1 teaspoon pepper
1/2 teaspoon marjoram optional

Melt butter or margarine in large frying pan and saute onion and celery until soft. Mix with remaining ingredients and toss well. Pack in large crock pot. Cover. Cook on high for 45 minutes, then turn to low and continue cooking for 6-8 hours.

German Apple Raisin Dressing

Mary Keyes' mother watched her German mother-in-law prepare this many times before the amounts were carefully measured and written down. Keyes prepares this each Thanksgiving, making four times the amount for a family that began with 11 children. Any other time of the year, a single recipe should be perfect to stuff a small bird for an average meal.

5 cups dry bread broken into pieces
1 1/2 cups water
5 cups sliced apples
1 cup raisins
1 1/2 teaspoons cinnamon
1 teaspoon allspice
1 teaspoon salt
2 eggs, slightly beaten

Sprinkle dry bread with water. Mix all ingredients together and stuff chicken or turkey.

CORN FRITTERS

A bundle of mail with corn fritter recipes arrived within a week of the initial request. Clara Reick first enjoyed these 50 years ago as a guest at the home of Fred and Elizabeth Risser of Madison.

1 egg
1 cup cream-style corn
1/2 cup cracker crumbs
1/2 teaspoon grated onion
1 Tablespoon melted butter
1/2 teaspoon salt and pepper
Bacon drippings or other oil for frying

Beat egg, add corn, cracker crumbs and onion, melted butter and seasonings. Drop by small spoonfuls into a frying pan in which 2 tablespoons bacon or similar fat have been melted. Brown on one side, turn and brown on other. Or the mixture may be fried by dropping small spoonfuls into deep fat heated to between 360 and 370 degrees.

Serves 4.

WILD GOOSE

A reader asked for a recipe for wild goose and within days this "tried and true" recipe arrived. It had been given years ago to Donna and Jack Thompson, Columbus, by Madison hunter Fred Friedig. For those of you who are planning a goose– rather than turkey– day, the Thompsons claim this to be "delicious."

One 3/4-ounce package brown gravy mix

1/4 cup flour

1 1/2 teaspoon salt

2 Tablespoons sugar

1 cup hot water

2 Tablespoons orange marmalade

1 (6-ounce) can orange juice concentrate, thawed

About 1 cup beer, optional

Combine all ingredients and put in large heavy-duty aluminum bag; place goose inside. Close loosely and put slots in top of bag. Cook about 3 hours at 350 degrees. (This can also work well in foil-lined roaster). Carve bird and pour sauce over to serve.

PUMPKIN POUND CAKE
WITH BUTTER SAUCE

Baked in a loaf pan, this cake will become an instant sweet hit in your home. The recipe was found in "The Pumpkin Eater's Cookbook" by Rosemary Smithson of the Pumpkin Patch in Verona.

1/2 cup firmly packed brown sugar

3/4 cup granulated sugar

3/4 cup shortening

2 eggs

1 cup pumpkin puree

1 3/4 cups unbleached flour, sifted

1 teaspoon salt

1 teaspoon baking soda

1 1/2 teaspoon cinnamon

1/4 teaspoon allspice

1/2 teaspoon nutmeg

1/2 cup chopped pecans (optional)

In large mixing bowl, combine sugars, shortening and eggs. Beat well on medium speed with electric mixer. Add pumpkin and continue beating for 1 minute more. Sift together the dry ingredients and gradually add them to the batter, beating 3 minutes at high speed. Stir in nuts and pour into well greased and floured 9x5x3-inch loaf tin. Bake in preheated oven at 350 degrees for 1 hour or until cake tests done. Serve with butter sauce.

BUTTER SAUCE:

1 cup butter

2 cups sugar

4 teaspoons flour

1 cup cream

1 teaspoon vanilla

Bring all but vanilla to a boil, remove from heat, then stir in vanilla. Serve warm over each serving.

Pumpkin Pound Cake

Janet Wendt wanted a pumpkin pound cake that was studded with raisins and nuts and was baked in a bundt pan. Barbara Fitzsimmons, Verona, sent this family favorite.

3 cups flour
2 teaspoons baking powder
1/2 teaspoon baking soda
2 teaspoons cinnamon
1 teaspoon allspice
1/2 teaspoon salt
1 cup salad oil
3 cups sugar
3 eggs
One (16-ounce) can pumpkin
1/2 cup or more chopped walnuts
1/2 cup or more raisins coated with a little flour

Sift dry ingredients and set aside. Blend well with an electric mixer the oil, sugar, then eggs, one at a time, beating well after each addition. Beat in pumpkin. Blend in dry ingredients until well mixed, before stirring in nuts and raisins. Pour into greased and floured tube or bundt pan. Bake at 350 degrees for 1 hour or until tested done. Leave plain, frost or make a sauce to pour over each serving.

PUMPKIN CHIFFON PIE

A reader called to request a pumpkin chiffon pie made without instant pudding or pie mix. My mind went directly to one passed on to me by my dear friend, Bette Brickson, who shared it for the first "Wisconsin Air and Army National Guard Officer's Wives Cookbook" that was published in the early 1970s.

3/4 cup brown sugar
1 envelope unflavored gelatin
1/2 teaspoon salt
1 teaspoon cinnamon
1/2 teaspoon nutmeg
1/4 teaspoon ginger
3 slightly beaten egg yolks
3/4 cup milk
1 1/4 cups canned pumpkin
3 egg whites
1/3 cup granulated sugar
One (9-inch) graham cracker crust

In saucepan combine brown sugar, gelatin, salt and spices. Combine egg yolks and milk; stir into brown sugar mixture. Cook and stir until mixture comes to boil. Remove from heat. Stir in pumpkin. Chill until mixture mounds slightly when spooned. Beat egg whites until soft peaks form. Gradually add granulated sugar, beating to stiff peaks. Fold pumpkin mixture thoroughly into egg whites. Turn into crust and chill until firm. Garnish with whipped cream, if desired.

SWEET POTATO-PECAN PIE

This recipe is from John Roussos, owner of New Orleans Take-Out. It is a sweet potato pie that will spoil you forever.

One 9-inch pie crust, unbaked
SWEET POTATO FILLING:
1 cup sweet potatoes or yams
1/4 cup packed brown sugar
1 Tablespoon white sugar
1 egg
1 Tablespoon cream
1 Tablespoon melted butter
1 Tablespoon vanilla
1/4 teaspoon cinnamon
1/4 teaspoon allspice
1/8 teaspoon nutmeg
1/4 teaspoon salt
PECAN MIXTURE:
3 eggs
1 cup sugar
1/2 cup dark corn syrup
2 Tablespoons melted butter
2 teaspoons vanilla
Pinch of cinnamon
Pinch of salt
3/4 cup pecans, whole or pieces (more if desired)

Preheat oven to 350 degrees. Bake sweet potato or yam, cool, skin and mash. Mix with brown sugar, white sugar, egg, cream, melted butter and vanilla. Sprinkle cinnamon, allspice, nutmeg and salt over sweet potato mixture and blend thoroughly. Spread with spatula into bottom of 9-inch pie crust, smooth evenly. Beat 3 eggs. Add 1 cup sugar and beat together. Add 1/2 cup dark corn syrup and beat. Add 2 Tablespoons melted butter and 2 teaspoons vanilla and blend. Add a pinch each of cinnamon and salt. Add pecans. Pour mixture over sweet potato filling. Cover surface with more pecans, if desired. Bake 50 minutes to an hour at 350 degrees. If pie browns too rapidly, reduce heat to 325 degrees. Center should be firm when pie is shaken.

Pumpkin Date Torte

One of my all-time favorites, clipped from a 1964 Better Homes and Gardens magazine.

1/2 cup chopped dates
1/2 cup chopped walnuts
2 Tablespoons flour
1/4 cup butter or margarine
1 cup brown sugar
2/3 cup cooked pumpkin (not quite a full can)
1 teaspoon vanilla
2 eggs
1/2 cup sifted all-purpose flour
1/2 teaspoon baking powder
1/2 teaspoon cinnamon
1/2 teaspoon nutmeg
1/4 teaspoon ginger
1/4 teaspoon baking soda

Mix dates, nuts and 2 tablespoons flour; set aside. Melt butter over low heat; blend in brown sugar. Remove from heat; stir in pumpkin and vanilla. Beat in eggs, one at a time. Sift together dry ingredients; add to pumpkin mixture, mixing thoroughly. Stir in floured dates and nuts; turn into greased 9x1 1/2-inch round baking pan. Bake at 350 degrees for 20 to 25 minutes. Serve warm with whipped cream.

Makes 8 servings.

Carlson's Dime Store's second location on East
Washington Avenue – near Union Corners.

Happy Holidays

······································· •

Roasted Chestnuts? Oyster stew? Shopping with grandchildren? Tchaikovsky's "Nutcracker?" It is that special time of the year when family customs begin to take on a myriad of images exuding the very essence of what makes a gentle glow within. The elements of the Midwest add to poinsettias, creches, candles, hymns, mistletoe and holly, gatherings, sharing, ethnicity and food, each merely skimming the surface of a long and cherished list of emotional yearly repeats.

In Paul Schlereth's home, holiday tradition means Grandma's anise-flavored German Springerle and hard candy, both made in Grandpa's homemade cast aluminum molds. It is an important part of Schlereth's heritage, and learning about it absorbed a portion of an afternoon visit, but only after renewing a friendship that began in 1953 when Schlereth and his wife, Bernice, became my first employers at their "dime" store on East Washington Avenue at Union Corners. Bernice's father, Ohio entrepreneur Albin Carlson, arrived in Madison in 1939, saw the dance floor in the Brueske building where the Cathay House is located today, then created a new plan for it. Schlereth would eventually be part owner of four Carlson's Dime Stores in the city, but thoughts during our recent reunion centered around the first location and a Christmas season during World War II.

Christmas tree lights were scarce and times were rough, so Schlereth offered his customers a replacement for each burned-out bulb. A police officer stood at the front door to keep order while people gathered in the cold to take advantage of the generous offer. He remembers the burned-out bulbs being beautifully colored, many shaped like birds and other creatures. At the end of the day, instead of discarding them, Schlereth carried the assortment home in a bag, tied a string around each bulb stem, then hung them as ornaments on the branches of his Christmas tree. It was a time he will never forget. Springerle also remains vivid in his mind—German cookies his mother, Hazel, made each December. It's a tradition carried on today, but somehow lacking the perfection of the past. Bubbles appear, erasing the intricate design carved by his father, John, in each square of religious and animal impression. Back then Grandmothers seemed to have a bit of magic in their fingertips that awaits duplication in the festive seasons of today.

HAZEL SCHLERETH'S SPRINGERLE

12 eggs
3 pounds powdered sugar
3 pounds sifted flour
3 scant teaspoons baking soda
Butter the size of 3 walnuts
Pure anise oil extract
Anise seeds

Separate eggs and beat whites and yolks separately for 10 minutes. Combine eggs and add sugar; beat an additional 10 minutes. Add anise extract to taste and smell. Sift flour and baking soda and add to egg mixture a little at a time. Use mixer until stiff, then stir by hand. Sprinkle about 1 teaspoon of anise seeds on a hard surface and roll out a portion of dough like a pie crust, about 1/4-inch thick. Additional seeds can be sprinkled over the dough before pressing mold. Repeat with remaining dough. Press molds on dough and cut apart with a rippled-edge pizza cutter. After cutting apart, place on a folded bedsheet to dry overnight. Dust off flour and turn over before going to bed. In the morning, bake on very lightly greased trays for 20 to 25 minutes at 275 degrees. A smaller version would call for 4 eggs, 2 pounds powdered sugar, 1 pound sifted flour, scant teaspoon baking soda, butter the size of a walnut; proceed as above.

Brandy Balls

What would the holidays be without tins of cookies and candy? Diane Calhoun, Barneveld, asked for a brandy ball recipe similar to what she was treated to in the 1960s in Baltimore, MD. This was discovered in Marian Hoffman's cookbook, "Creative Cooking Desserts," just in time for Christmas sampling at the Calhoun's.

One (6-ounce) package semisweet chocolate chips
One (5-ounce) can evaporated milk
2 1/2 cups cookie crumbs
1 cup sifted powdered sugar
1 cup coarsely chopped pecans
1/3 cup brandy
Chocolate sprinkles, ground nuts, flaked coconut and/or powdered sugar are suggestions for coatings.

Combine chocolate chips and milk in 2-quart saucepan; cook over low heat, stirring constantly, just until chocolate is melted and mixture is well-blended. Remove from heat. In bowl, combine cookie crumbs, powdered sugar, pecans and brandy; add to melted chocolate mixture.

Mix well. Refrigerate 30 minutes. Shape mixture into 1-inch balls; roll each in chocolate sprinkles or any of the other suggested coatings. Let finished brandy balls air-dry for 1 to 2 hours; store refrigerated in airtight container. Bring to room temperature before serving. Variation: To make raisin-rum balls, soak 1/2 cup seedless raisins in 1/3 cup rum; drain well and mix into other ingredients. Use rum in place of brandy in recipe as directed.

Makes 4 dozen.

Amish Velveeta Fudge

When William Jurs, Cambridge, asked for a fudge recipe made with Velveeta cheese, I was stumped. Otto Anderson, Madison, answered the call with this recipe he found in an Amish cookbook.

1 pound plain Velveeta cheese
1 pound butter
1 teaspoon vanilla
4 pounds confectioners' sugar
1 cup cocoa
1 cup coconut or nuts, optional

Over low heat in large pan, melt cheese, butter and vanilla together. Sift together sugar and cocoa and stir in optional coconut or nuts. Pour into buttered 9x13-inch pan. When firm, cut and slice. Keep refrigerated. Makes 6 pounds of fudge.

Note: This can be reduced to half and placed in an 8x8-inch pan. Note: Another recipe for a cheese fudge arrived from Mary Jane Anderson who substitutes cream cheese for Velveeta cheese because she prefers the flavor:

1 pound butter
1 pound cream cheese
1 cup cocoa
1 Tablespoon vanilla
4 pounds confectioners' sugar
1 cup chopped nuts

Melt butter and cheese over low heat. Remove from stove, add cocoa and vanilla. Beat until smooth. Add sugar and nuts; mix well. Spread or pat into two 9x13-inch lightly buttered pans, or one large cookie sheet with sides. Refrigerate for several hours to set.

Note: By using cream cheese, flavors other than chocolate can be introduced to your liking.

BROCCOLI HERB AND CHEESE BAKE

When the house swells with overnight guests during the holiday season, prepare this casserole the evening before to pop in the oven for a breakfast to remember. It is a favorite at Annie Stewart's Annie's House on the Hill Bed & Breakfast overlooking Warner Park. Fresh herbs from the herb garden make the house smell absolutely delicious.

EGG MIXTURE:
6 large eggs, beaten
1/4 cup bread crumbs
1/2 teaspoon fresh chopped oregano
1/2 teaspoon fresh chopped rosemary
1/2 teaspoon fresh chopped sage
1/2 teaspoon fresh chopped thyme
Pinch of salt, pepper
1 cup skim milk

OTHER INGREDIENTS:
12 ounces grated sharp Cheddar cheese
1 1/2 cups crisp cooked broccoli flowerettes
1/4 cup sauteed chopped onions
1/4 cup fresh chopped parsley
1/2 cup Cheddar cheese-flavored croutons
Sprinkle of paprika

Layer in buttered casserole as follows: Spread 3/4 of the Cheddar cheese evenly on bottom of dish. Next comes a layer of broccoli flowerettes, then chopped onion, and lastly chopped parsley, then, croutons. Sprinkle with paprika. Now, pour egg mixture over all. Sprinkle remaining cheese on top. Can be covered and stored in refrigerator until morning baking. Bake in a preheated oven at 300 degrees for 1 hour, 15 minutes. Let rest for about five minutes before cutting into six portions, pie-style. Serve with a slab of browned ham and homemade whole wheat bread or muffins to raves from your family and guests.

GRANDMA MARTY'S CHRISTMAS SALAD

When this recipe was submitted, Grandma Marty was 99 years old with a lifetime of memories. As a resident of the New Glarus Home, she enjoyed reminiscing about the past when she busied herself in the kitchen to prepare for family feasts. Her marshmallow salad was a favorite then, and still is.

    1/2 pound marshmallows
    3 egg yolks
    1/4 cup milk
    2 Tablespoons lemon juice
    1 large can fruit cocktail, drained well, saving juice
    4 Tablespoons fruit cocktail juice
    Pinch of salt; 2 cups whipped cream
    1/2 pound marshmallows, cut up
    1 cup white grapes, cut in half.

Place 1/2 pound marshmallows, egg yolks, 1/4 cup milk, lemon juice, fruit cocktail juice and salt in top of double boiler and cook until marshmallows are melted. Set aside until cold. Whip 2 cups cream. Add the cold marshmallow mixture. Add well-drained can of fruit cocktail, 1/2 pound of cut-up marshmallows and white grapes. Refrigerate overnight.

Note: Coat a large spoon scantily with butter so marshmallows will not stick when stirring in double boiler.

Acorn Squash Soup with Raspberry-Cranberry Glaze Jacobi's, Hazelhurst, WI.

Ginny Williams visited Jacobi's restaurant in Hazelhurst, near Minocqua, and wondered if they would part with this recipe. Owners Pam and Allan Jacobi and their sous-chef Kathy Larsen replied immediately. The name alone stirs a delectable image.

1 Tablespoon chopped garlic
1 large diced onion
1/2 cup butter
1/2 cup flour
2 quarts chicken stock
4 pounds pureed acorn squash
1 Tablespoon nutmeg
1 quart heavy whipped cream
Salt and pepper to taste

Saute garlic and onion in butter, add flour to form a paste, then add chicken stock and stir until thickened. Add squash, nutmeg and cream. Season with salt and pepper to taste.

Garnish with raspberry-cranberry glaze:
6 ounces frozen raspberries
1 cup frozen cranberries
2 cups water
1 cup sugar
1 Tablespoon cinnamon
1 teaspoon nutmeg
1 teaspoon allspice
1 Tablespoon cornstarch

Mix the above ingredients together and boil until thickened. garnish over squash.

RED CABBAGE

Proud of their German heritage, Fred and Kathy Voll were happy to share their Old World cooking secrets . . .

3 Tablespoons butter

1 large onion, diced

1 large jar of German red cabbage (see note)

1 or 2 medium sized apples, finely grated

1 bay leaf

1 or 2 Tablespoons honey

1 or 2 cloves, optional

3/4 to 1 cup beef stock or one bouillon cube dissolved in water

1/4 cup white or red wine, not too dry

Salt and pepper to taste

Melt butter; add diced onion and saute until pale yellow. Add red cabbage, apple, bay leaf, honey, cloves and stock. Slowly simmer until tender, 1 to 1 1/2 hours. Season to taste. Thicken with cornstarch blended with a small amount of water. Bring to a boil until thick. Now add wine to bring out red color and enhance taste. Serve. (Recipe from the Volls family of the Bavaria Sausage Kitchen, 6317 Nesbitt Road.)

Note: Red cabbage, available at the Bavaria Sausage Kitchen and other stores that offer German foods, can be placed in oven along with sauerbraten and simmered. The cooking time is about the same.

SAUERKRAUT

This is another holiday favorite from the Volls and their Bavaria Sausage Kitchen on Nesbitt Road

1 large can of German Winekraut

1 onion, diced

1 apple, peeled and diced

2 bay leaves

4 or 5 juniper berries

2 or 3 whole peppercorns

1 1/2 Tablespoons honey

4 slices bacon, cut in small strips, lightly fried with drippings

1 1/2 cups water

1 raw potato, grated

1/8 teaspoon caraway seed, optional

Place first nine ingredients in large pot. Bring to a boil. Simmer for one hour. Add finely grated potato and caraway, if being used, simmer for another 30 minutes. Delicious served with rouladen, sauerbraten, sausages, meals with pork, and on Reuben sandwiches.

SWEDISH MEATBALLS

My very dear friend, Clare Quale, and her mother, Irene Paulson, would prepare hundreds of Swedish meatballs each year in the kitchen of the Quale farm near Stoughton. After the meatballs had baked in a thick spicy gravy, they were frozen for last minute celebrations and family gatherings. Clare died in September 1992 and this recipe is in her memory.

1 pound ground beef and 1/4 pound of lean pork, ground together 3 or 4 times

  1 egg, beaten
  1 Tablespoon cornstarch
  1/2 cup milk
  1 small onion, minced fine
  1/8 teaspoon nutmeg;
  1/8 teaspoon allspice
  1/8 teaspoon ginger

Beat egg, then add remaining ingredients and stir well before mixing into meat. Roll into balls the size of a walnut and fry in butter until brown. Place in an oven roaster. Make gravy in fry pan with flour, drippings and water. Pour over meatballs. Cover and bake at 350 degrees for about 45 minutes. Note: Have a bowl of water handy to moisten hands to prevent sticking while rolling mixture into meatballs.

Note: If you plan to double, triple or make 10 times the amount, be careful with the amounts of milk used to keep the mixture from getting too soft.

Honey Cranberry Bread—
Wallace Honey Farm

Henry Wallace was 15 when he first became interested in beekeeping. In 1994, he celebrated his 50th anniversary as an apiarist and was happy to share a few recipes from his collection at his honey farm in Sullivan, Wis.

3/4 cup honey
1/4 cup butter
2 eggs
1 cup orange juice
1/4 cup milk powder
2 cups whole wheat flour
1 teaspoon baking powder
1 teaspoon baking soda
1/2 teaspoon salt
2 cups fresh chopped cranberries
1 cup chopped nuts

Cream honey and butter. Beat in eggs and orange juice. Sift together dry ingredients; gradually add to mixture. Fold in cranberries and nuts. Pour into two loaf pans, oiled and floured. Bake at 325 degrees for 1 1/2 hours or until done. Cool about 10 minutes before removing from pans.

Tom Thumb Fruitcakes

I love fruitcake! This recipe can be baked in a 10-inch tube pan, or in muffin pans for 38 individual cakes.

1 cup butter
1 cup sugar
4 eggs, one at a time
1 2/3 cups flour
1 1/2 teaspoons baking powder
1/2 teaspoon salt
1/4 cup pineapple juice
2 cups coarsely chopped hazelnuts
1/2 pound white raisins
1 pound mixed candied fruit
8 ounces red glaze cherries
1/4 pound pitted chopped dates
1/4 pound dried chopped figs
1 cup drained crushed pineapple
1/3 cup flour

Cream butter and sugar, then add one at a time until well blended. Mix dry ingredients and add alternately to mixture with pineapple juice. Toss nuts and fruits with 1/3 cup flour and fold into mixture. Line 10-inch tube pan with double thickness of greased brown paper and bake at 300 degrees for 2 hours, 45 minutes. Cool in pan; remove. (Store in plastic in refrigerator.) Soak periodically with brandy or sherry. Makes one fruitcake.

Yield: 38 Tom Thumb fruitcakes.

Note: To make Tom Thumbs, line 2 1/2-inch muffin pans with papers, two liners each. Use 1/2 cup batter and top with nut-fruit mixture. Bake at 300 degrees for 1 hour.

Carrot Steamed Pudding with Lemon Sauce

Betty Scott, Madison, remembered the carrot steamed pudding that her stepmother's mother gave her as a gift every Christmas during the 1940s and 1950s. This was discovered in Jane Watson Hopping's delightful cookbook, "The Pioneer Lady's Country Christmas," filled with old-fashioned family recipes and memories of the past.

6 Tablespoons suet, finely ground
1/2 cup packed dark brown sugar
1 egg
1 Tablespoon water
1 cup finely grated carrots
1 cup white seedless raisins
2 teaspoons finely grated lemon peel
1 1/4 cups sifted cake flour
1 teaspoon baking powder
1 teaspoon ground cinnamon
1 teaspoon grated nutmeg
1/2 teaspoon baking soda
1/4 teaspoon ground cloves
1/2 teaspoon salt
1/4 teaspoon ground ginger

Purchase clean white suet at the butcher's or ask for it at the meat counter at your grocery store. Work the suet with a spoon until soft. Add the sugar, stirring together. Beat the egg with water and add to suet-sugar mixture; stir until blended. Stir in carrots, raisins and lemon peel. Gradually add the dry ingredients to suet-sugar mixture, stirring well. Turn into a greased and floured 1 1/2-quart pudding mold or can; fill no more than two-thirds full; cover. Set the mold in a deep saucepan with a wire rack fitted in the bottom. Pour enough boiling water in the saucepan to come about halfway up the sides of the mold. Cover saucepan and slowly bring to a boil, then reduce heat to maintain water at a simmer and steam for 2 hours. Unmold onto a serving platter. When pudding is almost cool, serve topped with lemon sauce.

Makes 10 to 12 servings.

LEMON SAUCE:

1 cup sugar

1/2 cup butter or margarine

1 Tablespoon cornstarch

1/2 cup water

1/2 cup strained lemon juice

Finely grated rind from 1 lemon

Combine the sugar and butter in the top of a double boiler. In a small bowl, dissolve the cornstarch in the water and lemon juice; add to the sugar-butter mixture. Stir in lemon rind. Bring sauce to a boil over medium heat, stirring almost constantly until sugar dissolves, butter melts and ingredients are well blended. Continue cooking until sauce is clear and thick, about 15 to 20 minutes more. Serve with pudding while still hot or when lukewarm.

Makes about 2 cups.

Suet Pudding Traditional Christmas Pudding, Jane Oke Prisk 1832-1907

Another response to Judy Gile's request came from Ruth Jungbluth, Dodgeville, with the recipe Jungbluth's great grandmother brought with her in 1854 from Cornwall, England, to Mineral Point, where she settled. Jungbluth continues with the tradition by preparing it a week or two before it is to be served, storing it in a cool place, then resteaming it on Christmas Day. Her husband's Yorkshire-bred family refers to the sauce as "dip." They sprinkle the pudding with brandy before wrapping it to mellow, and add brandy to the sauce. Great grandma never did. As an avowed teetotaler, she considered it to be a "demon."

1 1/2 cups sugar (all white or part white, part brown)
4 cups flour
1 teaspoon allspice
1 teaspoon cinnamon
1/2 teaspoon nutmeg
2 teaspoons baking powder
1 teaspoon salt
2 cups beef suet, finely chopped or ground
2 cups raisins
1 cup dried currants
2 to 2 1/2 cups water
6 ounces mixed candied fruit, optional

Mix dry ingredients in large bowl. Stir in finely chopped or ground suet. Add raisins, currants and fruit, if used. Mix well. Add water, part at a time, to make a stiff dough. Just moisten flour well. This is more like bread dough than cake batter. Place pudding in pan that fits inside another larger kettle (a 9 1/2x3-inch insert pan of an old-fashioned "waterless" cooker would work well, as would a 9 1/2-inch springform pan). If pan holding pudding doesn't hang inside larger pan, use a rack with legs, or overturned soup bowl to keep pudding pan above water level in larger kettle. A double-boiler won't work for this as rim separates inset pan from steam. Cover pudding dough lightly with waxed paper. Cover larger kettle with well-fitting lid. Steam 3 to 4 hours, adding water to larger pan as needed. Cool and store as instructed, or serve with pudding sauce. Leftover pudding can be reheated by steaming.

Note: Brandy can be sprinkled over steamed pudding to season it while it is being stored, or the pudding can be covered with a brandy-soaked towel.

PUDDING SAUCE:

1 cup white sugar

1 cup brown sugar

6 Tablespoons cornstarch

1/2 teaspoon cinnamon

1/4 teaspoon nutmeg

2/3 cup butter

3 to 4 cups hot water

Mix together dry ingredients. Cut in butter. Stir in hot water. Heat and stir in top pan of double boiler until clear and smooth, adding water as needed to make sauce desired consistency.

Note: Can omit cinnamon and nutmeg and instead add 1 1/2 teaspoons lemon extract to sauce with hot water. Or, if desired, brandy or rum may be added to sauce before serving.

INDEX

CAKES, COOKIES, FROSTINGS, DESSERTS